14 flys y Fel...

Hear the Train Blow

The classic autobiography
of growing up in the bush

PATSY ADAM-SMITH

PENGUIN BOOKS

Penguin Books Australia Ltd
487 Maroondah Highway, PO Box 257
Ringwood, Victoria 3134, Australia
Penguin Books Ltd
Harmondsworth, Middlesex, England
Viking Penguin, A Division of Penguin Books USA Inc.
375 Hudson Street, New York, New York 10014, USA
Penguin Books Canada Limited
10 Alcorn Avenue, Toronto, Ontario, Canada M4V 3B2
Penguin Books (N.Z.) Ltd
182-190 Wairau Road, Auckland 10, New Zealand

First published by Thomas Nelson Australia 1964
Expanded illustrated edition published 1981
Paperback edition 1987
This edition published by Penguin Books Australia Ltd 1992

9 10 8

Made and printed in Australia by Australian Print Group, Maryborough

National Library of Australia
Cataloguing-in-Publication data

Adam-Smith, Patsy
Hear the train blow.

ISBN 0 14 016538 X.

1. Adam-Smith, Patsy. 2. Authors, Australian - 20th
century - Biography. 3. Country life - Victoria - Waaia. I. Title.

A828.309

CONTENTS

PROLOGUE

I n some ways childhood is in all ways the age of innocence; later we may learn that it was our age of ignorance or, worse still, the time when we knew everything but could turn a blind eye on the sufferings of others, the greed, the lust, the sacrifice and the dishonour that goes to make up everyday life. But overall, our recollections are of the good times – interspersed with the horrible times when things didn't suit us alone.

Hear the Train Blow is a true story. The names of two minor families have been altered; that is all. The rest is as it happened during the Great Depression as we, the 'respectable poor', lived through the worst of times, the best of times. Like most lives, the living of it seemed the most natural, the only *real* way to live. All our closest friends lived and worked on railways; three of my aunts, my mother's sisters, were in charge of railway stations or post offices in places as isolated as were we, and other aunts waited on small, hungry farms in Gippsland for their railway-fencer husbands to come home from the little cabin on wheels shunted into a lonely siding.

Because we were busy getting on with life it didn't even seem hilarious at the time that the struggling dairy farmers, such as my mother's family, looked on the timber-getters from the hills, such as Dad's family, as 'wild' and undisciplined; and those free, independent men of the tall timber country looked with disdain on the time-imprisoned 'cow-cockies'.

Dad's father and his brothers (there were eight boys until World War I) were said to have cut more railway sleepers than any other family in Australia. 'Those Smith boys were all born with a broad axe in their hands,' they used to say in the Gippsland forests back of Neerim.

When looking through my mother's Box Brownie album for material for the illustrated edition of this book I found the newspaper advertisement for the brown overcoat in which she so proudly posed, standing in our garden at Monomeith: 2s 6d a week for £8 10s 0d worth of weeks, 36 weeks. It was 1934 and the opposite page of *The Leader* was wholly taken up with the weddings of the year: Hordern–Bailleau, Brooks–Gengoult Smith and Haynes–Syme. We were so far removed from the city, the social scene, the mores and movements of the age that these would truly have been reports from another world. In 1934 little girls were 'in' as bridal attendants. 'The most photographed little girlie, Marguerite Manifold, had to be carried over the heads of the crowds that thronged outside the church to get a glimpse of the bride.' And ostentation was the rule: 'Seven bridesmaids for the Haynes–Syme wedding were dressed alike in blue and white, copies of the Romney picture *The Age of Innocence*. The groom's gifts to the seven bridesmaids were bracelets of platinum, turquoise and pearls. The bride's mother's frock was of brown ring velvet, the deep wide cuffs of Kolinsky fur lined with gold tissue.'

There was no bitterness in our reading of this. If they did not know we were out there in the bush in our home-made dresses and O'Gilpin's 'nothing over 2/6' pearl necklets we just as casually took no notice of them down there 'dolled up in feathers and fur-belows', as Mick would have said. That the power of some families may influence or make or mar our lives was something we didn't speak of. If we knew it. Mum was innocent of such matters. All Dad ever said about wealth was, 'We mightn't have much money but we can have a lot of fun.' And we did.

It was the sort of fun that made a firm padding around the body of the spirit and cushioned you when you left home and shut your eyes and jumped into the boxing ring.

Like many another I learnt a lot about myself while serving during the war. Not that I had a hard war – on the contrary. I was with one of the most interesting and newest hospitals in the army, the First Australian Orthopaedic Unit. Bone banks were new, bone grafts almost as new; much of the skill of our surgeons and physiotherapists had been perfected during the poliomyelitis outbreak of the late 1930s; we were a small, compact unit that travelled together around the eastern States, set up our tents, unpacked our equipment, cleaned up and worked and spent our time off together. We remain friends to this day. But there is a level ground each of us finds when catapulted into living with a crowd, an unmoving place where we can live a life apart, but not alone, or set up as a stage and present ourselves as we wish the world to see us and thus keep intact our deep private self.

Then the church bells rang out all over the land and we ran up and down the streets of Australia shouting 'It's over! The boys will be coming home!', or we crouched in a corner crying for the boys who wouldn't be coming home and praying for the boys we hoped were alive and would be discovered in POW camps.

From the noisy, happy, sad, tragic, brave and fearful world of hospitals full of young men where I fitted so well, I went to live in Tasmania. For a writer this was virgin country. From that day of my first flight, when I got off the long, backless, wooden stools in the army plane and jumped down onto that island, I knew I would write and write and write. Over 300 feature articles for national magazines poured out, as did radio serials for children under seven (little children before education cramped their imagination and mental courage), short stories – the writing form I prefer – radio talks, and later guest speaking engagements.

Then Kylie Tennant befriended me. By now I was at sea. Literally. I had again shut my eyes and jumped, this time onto a tramp trader, and for six years sailed as deck-hand, cook–radio operator, first on a 60-tonner and then on a 300-ton wooden ship from the Port of Hobart to islands off the Tasmanian east coast and Bass Strait. By the time I met Kylie I'd seen men die, heard one dying and couldn't help him, lived hard, and worked too hard. I'd been with CSIRO teams banding birds on uninhabited islands, camped with leading artists and scientists, made many overland journeys on 'The Mainland', as Tasmanians call it; some journeys I drove 'the whole way round' Australia, others were shorter trips to the inland of six or seven thousand miles. I'd been to much of the back country; I'd camped with Aborigines for seven winters when my lung turned sulky and I needed to escape Tasmania's winter.

'Mary Woollong would have fixed you up,' Dad had said, half-joking, to cover his concern for my health and half-suggesting a possible remedy. But Mary Woollong, whom we had known at Nowingi when I was small, had now died with the sad title of 'the last of the Kulkyne tribe'. The thought of the days when I had run as a child beside her on the red sandhills out in Sunset Country and breathed in the dry, sweet desert air sent me off north of 26 degrees, and there the dispossessed tribesmen befriended me until soon I was ready to take on the world once again.

Sometimes I've knuckled down to indoor work, such as advising and enrolling Adult Education students in Hobart for six years, and then I was offered the position in Melbourne of Manuscripts' Field Officer, the first such position in Australia, to search the country for historic documents, letters, diaries, property and family records and encourage the owners to deposit them in the State Library of Victoria as a donation to the State and, ultimately, the Nation.

'You must get these experiences into books,' Kylie ordered. 'You've known Australians and Australia like few of us can. Write it!'

So my real time has been spent writing about the ordinary – extraordinary? – women and men of our land, the timber-getters, farmers, bushmen, railwaymen, seamen, Aborigines, battlers and the legendary generation of World War I. Sometimes I think, fleetingly, of going back to music, of university, but I don't think like that for long. I leave these things to those who have never heard the steam whistle blow and great engines thunder past our simple homes in the bush, a sound and a smell that can shunt you back to your own childhood and that of a nation.

When I set to work to write *Hear the Train Blow* I wondered how I should go about it. In 1960 I was more sophisticated, no longer the 'bush rat' that the Man in Grey on Spencer Street railway station once called me. But then I remembered Mr Martin, our neighbour long ago. He used 'big' words and one night playing cribbage he said to my mother, 'So you come from Gippsland, Mrs Smith. That is very undulating country.' After he left for his home Mum said, 'Why couldn't he say hilly?' He was known to us from that night on as 'Undulating Martin'. And I recalled the thin young woman at Waaia who had nothing good to say of anyone. She was known as 'Vinegar Lips'. Such memories guided my style for this, my first book. But that was after I began it.

What happened was this: after Kylie had cajoled me into 'getting experiences into books' I wrote a long account – 500 pages – of my years at sea, the ships and the island people. I didn't show it to anyone. It was as though I was waiting for something else. And then it came: I sat down and began to write the story of my childhood and the fear that hovered like a wraith about me, and of Mum and Dad and Miss Mickie. I finished it in three weeks and sent it off to Ure-Smith and they published it as it was. (The long work on my years at sea fell into two halves that later became *Moonbird People* and *There Was a Ship*.)

It is not immodest of me to say that *Hear the Train Blow* was a success. It was called 'a minor classic' by Kenneth Slessor. Lord Casey wrote to me, 'Everyone will think they can write of their childhood after reading your book. Writing simply looks so easy.' Nearly thirty years later I am still receiving letters from all over Australia and from England and Ireland.

The first letter I received was from May Asquith from Euroa in Victoria. 'I saw the book advertised,' she wrote. 'I thought, I never heard of anyone writing a book about ordinary people like us before. So I bought it. It was the second book I've bought in my life. The other was the Book of Common Prayer. They were both great investments.' May Asquith and I still correspond.

I sent a copy to Mum. I waited. There was no word. The reviews, letters, warm messages from readers were nothing if Mum didn't care for it. Then her letter arrived.

'Some of the things you wrote were very hurtful. But so much was very beautiful. And we love you for being honest. And we love you.' The truth of the matter was that that was all that mattered.

PREFACE:
DOWN AT
THE STATION

The troop train was so long that when we'd got through
the checking barriers with our kitbags, tin helmets, gas
masks and the rest of our gear we had to walk the length
of ten carriages before we reached those set aside for nurses.
Now, four hours later, we were all aboard – the soldiers, sailors,
airmen, nursing sisters and us enlisted Voluntary Aid Detach-
ments. The engine attempting to move off with us made slow
progress.

Over on No. 2 Platform the civilians who had waited
patiently for the four hours now began to wave and sing. 'You
are my sunshine,' they sang. Most of the nurses and many of
the men had parents and friends there to wave them goodbye.
I looked out on to the now empty No. 1 Platform. It was as

I knew it best.

'Do you know Spencer Street railway station?' our kindly matron had asked before we left on final leave.

'Yes, matron,' I nodded solemnly. 'I know Spencer Street.'

The Man in Grey, that mine of information of the Victorian Railways, spoke a final warning into his microphone and his voice resounded down the platform along the crowded carriages. 'Train leaving Number One Platform. Stand clear, please, stand clear.' Then, 'God bless you, boys, and a safe return.' He left his little box then, his day's work done, and walked across to the iron railing and watched us go. His eyes met mine as the train slowly passed. I waved.

'Goodbye, sweetheart,' the old man called.

'Goodbye,' I replied. I thought perhaps he remembered me. I took off my hat with the badge of St John of Jerusalem on it so he would see my ink-black hair that he once had remarked on.

'Goodbye,' I called again.

'Goodbye,' he called back, and began walking along outside the iron railing, keeping abreast of my window. The civilians on No. 2 Platform were now singing, 'Wish me luck as you wave me goodbye.'

'Good luck, girlie,' the Man in Grey called as he kept pace with the train. For a moment I hesitated – could he tell I wasn't yet eighteen? No one else had . . . 'Good luck,' he called again. I laughed, the train was gathering speed now and as it got faster the wheels began to sing:

Tallygaroopna, Tallygaroopna,
Ho, Ho, Tallygaro . . .

We had passed the end of the platform. I leant out and the wind of the train's movement blew the hair across my eyes. 'Goodbye,' I cried. He took his peaked cap off and waved it, the only man left on the long platform, standing there waving until we were swallowed up.

WORKING ON THE RAILWAY

My parents were railway people and we lived beside the tracks all our life.

My mother was station and postmistress of lonely places where often our house was all there was of the town named on the railway signpost. Sometimes our four-roomed wooden cottage was on the platform and as we lay asleep the great steam engines crunched by like nailed boots crossing our bedroom floor.

My father wore the badge of the navvy, the scarred hands and leathered neck of a lifetime of toil on the tracks where pick, shovel and 28-pound hammer were the only tools of trade.

My sister played groom to me as horse in trucks that were shunted into our playground, the siding, for all the years until it was time for her to take over as station-mistress.

In those days before TV, radio and even electricity came to our harsh areas on the edge of the outback, we talked and listened a lot. We spent cold desert nights in front of our red-gum sleeper fire and in summer, after mirage-hot days, we sat outside watching the stars slide across the big sky and taking in the lore of our household. Stories were told and retold, embellished or honed down to polish them in the mould of all traditions. If the telling one night did not excite or interest the listeners, the next night the emphasis would be different, the timing, the tone, the silences altered. But always the core remained constant. In this way, by the time the child was conscious of telling the story herself she had become melded into the people, the land and the movements of the stars; time wavered and it was as though she took part in the events and ages that were in reality her grandmothers', her parents' time.

The story of my being was like this. It always seemed that I took part in, saw, heard, fretted at, laughed at the coming of the baby that was me. I'd heard it often enough to know it by heart. When I was five days old my mother took me by train from Spencer Street away from Melbourne where I was born up into the Mallee where my father waited for us.

Dad worked on the line as a fettler; his section was the flat long miles skirting the Hattah Desert country at Nowingi. My mother was station-mistress cum postmistress at Nowingi. This office served Kulkyne cattle station, twelve miles away. As far as the eye could see there was only one house besides ours, that of another fettler and his wife. This woman looked after the office when Mum was in Melbourne. In the crowded, laughter-filled days of childhood I never thought it strange that Mum should go down only one day before my arrival and return as soon as I could travel. She wrote to Dad from Melbourne. Two days later the engine-driver pulled his train up when he saw the gang at the side of the track.

'Where's Albert Smith?' he called. A letter had come in the mailbag and the fettler's wife at Nowingi had sent it up to him.

Everyone knew he was awaiting news of the baby. The driver climbed down from his hot cab onto the track and delivered the letter. He waited while Dad read it aloud.

Squatting beside the railway line on the red soil of that red, dusty land where the desert meets the acres man has claimed, he read from my mother's letter to his mates, some standing nearby rolling cigarettes, another tinkering with the motor of the Casey Jones.

'The baby,' he read, 'was born on the thirty-first of May, has black, curly hair, weighs eight pounds, and should not be upset by the long journey home.' The men laughed. 'When are you going to wet its head, Albert?' My father wasn't a drinking man, but today was different. He asked the driver to bring him a billy of beer on the run back the next day. 'I'll fix you up for it then.' Fettlers never carried money, or, as Dad said, never had any to carry.

Next day on the way back the engine was pulled up and the driver and guard climbed down carrying a black billy of beer each. The fireman followed them, mopping his neck with his sweat-rag. 'It's as hot as the hobs of hell up there today,' he said, and nodded up to where the heat shimmered in his cab. When all the mugs were full Kelly the ganger lifted his and said, 'To Albert's son. May he be half the man his father is.' 'Good luck to you, Albert,' the others toasted him. They drank the flat, warm beer, one mug apiece, and the driver and the fireman climbed back on the engine. The guard stood beside the track ready to jump onto the step when his van came by.

'I'll have him up here on the footplate in a few years,' the driver called down.

'I might nab him first,' said the guard. 'Make a shunter out of him.' When the train had rumbled off, blowing a congratu-latory cock-a-doodle-doo on its whistle, the gang picked up their crowbars and returned to their toil. As the men heaved in unison, levering a new rail up, Kelly said, 'They've got Buckley's chance. We'll keep your kid in the gang.'

'Too right!' said the men.

When Mum arrived and they found I was a girl they were just as happy.

'A little dancing partner,' the bachelor ganger said. Any sort of baby was a novelty to them. There wasn't another white infant for twenty miles. Had they been more experienced they would have seen nothing enchanting about this baby. I had been so ill all the way up I was in bad need of a bath; so was my mother because of me. In the privacy of the little four-roomed wooden house she told Dad, 'She's been crying all the way, food coming up, pants to be changed. I don't know what to do. I'm alarmed for her.' The train had left Spencer Street at 6 p.m. and had not arrived till the afternoon of the following day. It had jolted slowly, sickeningly, the 300-odd miles. The night had been bitterly cold.

'I put the small thing under my coat near my body to keep her warm,' Mum said, as if to prove that nothing she had done had brought on this debility. 'Time and again when the train stopped I went to the engine and got water from the driver. But she couldn't keep even boiled water down.'

The gang had organised their work to be near Nowingi when the train arrived. Now Dad went out and told them the baby was ill. She must be taken to the baby health centre at Red Cliffs, twenty miles up the line.

Kelly the ganger took Mum and me on the popping Casey Jones while Dad jogged off with our horse and jinker to pick us up from Carwarp on our way home. Here, ten miles from our home, the ganger lived. The wind was dry and strong as the Casey exploded its way along, and ganger Kelly took off his big black velour hat that had no dent in the crown and held it above my head to keep off the sun.

'I'll shelter her with me hat,' he shouted above the motor.

The clinic was sterile, antiseptic, and smelt of soap, carbolic acid and fresh fly-spray. Kelly held the door open, still trying to hold his hat above the baby's head and getting under Mum's feet all the way.

'Shut that door!' the clinic sister snapped. Kelly was noted for his whisper, which was reputed to be audible thirty feet away. Now he whispered. 'An old maid! I bet I know more about bringing up dingo pups than she does about babies.'

He may have been right, for when I was next presented at the clinic, weak, thin and puling, it was discovered I was dying of malnutrition. Mum thought I should have cow's milk, but the nurse insisted that I be kept on the powdered baby food she had recommended. On the way home on the Casey, Kelly burst out: 'Powdered milk! I was away from my camp once. A bloke, a careless sort of a cow I realised too late, he gave my wolfhound bitch powdered milk. Do you know what it did to her? Gave her worms!'

That night Dad set off across the roadless plain to Kulkyne homestead.

'Have you brought a halter?' said the cattleman when Dad told him of his sick baby.

Yes, he had a halter but 'About the money. I haven't any. I could come and see you on pay day.'

'That's all right. You better pick a sturdy little cow and get going. You've got a long walk ahead of you.' And Dad set off for home leading the sturdy little cow twelve miles over the stunted mallee growth in the night light.

In four weeks' time I was flourishing and this led Dad to claim proudly, 'Just shows what we who live in woop-woop can do when we try!' (Dad always subscribed to the belief that the poor come from 'woop-woop' and the affluent 'live on the land'.)

KATHLEEN-CUM-MICK

L ong before I learnt that babies were found beneath paddy-melon plants I thought that my sister Kathleen who was called Mick had been conceived in my mother's dream-world and moulded to life in her hands. My mother was psychic, gently so, yet often with an element of tragedy within her premonitions. Two years after their marriage she woke my father and said, 'I dreamt we had a baby. She had red hair and blue eyes but no clothes at all.' Dad teased her.

'You're sure it was our baby?'

'Yes, she called me Mummy.'

That afternoon there was a funeral in Warragul, where they then lived. Mum was returning from shopping when she saw it.

'It was very sad,' she told Dad. 'There was only one man and a priest walking behind the hearse. I wonder who the poor man was burying?'

It was his wife, the mother of his three tiny children. The priest told Mum when he called next day. The man was alone in Australia, had come from Ireland and couldn't find work. The family had been living in a tent and there the mother lost her life giving birth to a dead child.

'There's two small boys left and a tiny girl,' the priest said. 'Will you take the little girl?'

'Yes.' With no more hesitation than that Mick had a mother. That evening Mum told Dad.

'But our own children might come along some day,' he reasoned. 'Would it be kind to take a child that may later be less than one of our own?'

'When our babies come we'll have time enough to worry about that. In the meantime this is our baby.' Next day she went down to Pakenham, where the father lived. There, washed, waiting for her in the tent, was a red-haired, blue-eyed toddler. Her dress was freshly washed but threadbare.

'Has she no clothes?'

'No, that's all,' the man said. He was nursing the two little boys, one on each knee. Now he put them down and, kneeling to the earth, pulled a tin trunk from beneath the bed.

'Rita was making this. It was for Mickie. That's what we called Kathleen sometimes.' He handed her a tiny cream dress only half-finished, the needle and thread slipped in under the hem where it had been left by the woman now dead.

'What will you do with the boys?'

The man was vague with bereavement. He thought he would be able to care for the boys in the bush alone.

'But I'll miss my red-headed Mickie.'

Mum tried to console him. 'She'll miss you, too.'

'No, it's her mother she misses. Looks for her all the time.'

The little girl had not looked up. Now it was time to go and the man put his hand on her silky head and led her out into the sunlight. There in the clear light she suddenly saw . . . a woman's skirt. Stumbling on her little legs, without looking up she ran across and clutched it.

'Mummy,' she sobbed. 'It's Mummy.'

Mum lifted her up in her plump, warm arms and without looking back carried her across the paddocks to the railway station to wait for the train. Many years later she told us, 'She knew I wasn't her mother, but she so badly wanted me to be that she made herself believe. All the way home in the train she nuzzled into me whimpering "Mummy", over and over again. She didn't look up to my face once.

'From the moment she clutched my skirt she had hold of my heart. I was the one she needed. Love for her brought the desire and strength to protect her. I knew then that her father, no one, would ever take her from me.'

No one did. The lonely father never came to see her. Shortly after, he was found dead in the bush from a gunshot wound. He died alone.

Kathleen was seven years older than me. She was my father's favourite. She was a laugher, a girl without care, a dare-devil. Dad even named a racehorse after her, Miss Mickie. I didn't mind coming second best to Mick in Dad's affection. I loved him more for loving the things about her that I loved her for.

'Ginger Mick and Paddy-the-next-best-thing,' he'd introduce us, and I'd be proud. Mostly she was known as Mickie; Kathleen! only to be rebuked. (My name was Patricia Jean but I mostly got Jeanie.)

A Welsh stockman from Kulkyne station used to play 'bunyips' on the floor with Mick. His bodily contortions, facial grimaces and fearsome blood-curdling yells made me dislike the game, but Mick loved it.

'Who is this brave bunyip with the red hair?' he asked.

'That,' said Dad, 'that is Kathleen-cum-Mick.'

After his departure from Nowingi, Taffy wrote, sending his love to 'Kathleen-cym-Mick'.

THE WILD LIFE

The Mallee, that stretch of country in north-west Victoria, was being turned into a dust bowl by steam-driven 'mallee-rollers' and tree trunks dragged behind horse teams with heavy chains. They rolled down every tree, shrub, bush and plant and then grubbed out the stumps of the stunted trees and sold them in the cities as 'mallee-roots', leaving the top-soil to be blown away by the willy-willies, the Cock-Eye-Bobs that swept in off the desert during the hot summer months. The hot, dry winds whirled the dust up high as the sky where it travelled until it reached the coastal cities and fell on the streets and houses, and women ran around shutting doors and windows crying, 'Quick! It's a Mallee dust storm!' and we were nearly three hundred miles away from them.

The olive-green mallee scrub disappeared and left a land where emus, kangaroos and lizards up to six feet long were the only permanent residents in a temperature that could hover around 112°F for days at a time.

Before I could walk I knew of Reg Negri, a small, slightly built man who arrived to work on the rail track. The hard ganger of the time looked at him and said, 'You won't do. Get back on the train. You won't stand up to the work; it gets up to 112° in the shade here.' 'Who in the hell works in the shade?' little Negri snapped back. It was Reg Negri caused that ganger's transfer. I'd watched Dad coming in stooped at night from the track. 'He won't let us kneel down to weed,' he told Mum as she rubbed his back. 'Makes us stoop to weed the track. All day.' Then he came home one night. 'Little Negri took the big fellow on today. We'd swung the twenty-eight pound hammers all day straightening rails the heat had bent like a dog's hind leg, and then he says we had to work back to finish pulling weeds near the end of the track. "Bend your backs," he told us. "None of your loafing down on your knees." Little Negri watched the rest of us bend our backs and then he got down on his knees. The big fellow said he'd fire him. Negri said, "Tell that to the Road Foreman," and darned if he'd seen the inspection motor coming. We all kept working, Negri down on his knees, the rest of us cracking our backs. And what do you think the foreman said? He told us to all get on home and come back tomorrow and go down on our knees.' Dad was smiling away in that quiet way he had. 'I reckon we might have seen the last of The Kaiser.' They had. The ganger was transferred and dear old ganger Kelly came back. Dad always said Negri could have done his job in. 'He is a brave man that Negri, he's got courage.'

Our siding was on the line to Mildura but to the west, out in what some called The Great Desert and we knew as Sunset Country, a rail track was being built to nowhere. Well, that's where it ended. Nowadays on railway maps it is noted as 'The Nowingi towards Millewa South' and the sixteen miles of rails stop at a small gypsum mine. It had been planned to cross the dry Sunset Country to the South Australian border to serve the soldier settlers who came full of hope when the government rolled down the mallee and called it farmland. Then, as now, in this red, dusty land, the only words on maps west of Nowingi were Government Bore, or Salt Pans. Salt was gathered there for a time and one day Mum with her Box Brownie snapped a camel train laden with sixty bags of salt coming out of the desert and lumping towards the railway siding.

Two hundred construction navvies toiled to put down a track that the sand claimed as swiftly as they laid it. Their materials were hauled by 'The Red Terror', a goods wagon with a tractor engine mounted on top of it. On occasions the men came in on this to Nowingi and 'jumped' the train to Red Cliffs for a 'bout on the hops', as they said to Dad. Not that Dad could have much converse with these rovers of the construction world – Mum saw to that. 'Not a respectable married man among them, living like nomads, gambling their wages, getting drunk and belonging to no one anywhere.' Mum was the wife of a settled man and she saw to it that the wild lads of unfettered horizons got no chance of putting ideas into his head. The one thing the respectable fettlers had in common with the navvies up there was the sand. Here, where the sand had decayed to fine dust that sat across the land like a fixed cloud, Dad's gang was issued with industrial respirators, but Dad said he'd 'fly backwards like the crows do up here' rather than wear one.

When the men knocked off work on a Saturday they had to bring in everything movable; the more careless construction men once left their shovels and crowbars standing upright in a pyramid and when they returned on the Monday morning the tools, along with the line, were hidden under five feet of sand.

To defeat the sand blowing onto the track up in this country the innovative fettlers experimented with scores of gadgets. One, made of a curved sheet of galvanised iron which they called a Sunset Sand Chute, was placed beside the track in such a manner that the wind funnelling along it blew the sand straight up and over the rails to the other side of the track. They'd spend their lunch half-hour and weekends refining this device, such as making it narrower or angled differently to cause the sand to be blown at a greater speed, thus having it travel further from the line.

Nowingi was Mum's first post as station and postmistress. On being sent here she had been told that the relieving station-master would stay a few days to 'show her the ropes', such as despatching trains, decoding departmental telegrams and attending to post-office routine. But when she arrived the lad hopped on the departing train leaving a note under her office door, 'I am very sorry to do this to you Mrs Smith but I've been here six months. The last five families haven't stayed here long enough to get unpacked and even before I got here the past two families before that had applied for and got compassionate transfers to go anywhere at all rather than here.'

That was only one of the misfortunes in the first twenty-four hours there. During the morning, Belle, the Irish wolfhound dog Granddad Adams had had imported for Mum for hunting had got at a parcel of meat that had been thrown onto the platform from a passing train and had eaten the lot. It had been consigned to an Indian hawker who would call for it. By the time he arrived Mum had decided she must pay him for the loss. It took all the little money she had – and pay day was a fortnight away.

Belle, a romping great puppy the size of a Shetland pony (we kids used to ride her round the bush), set a fashion for those parts and several men sent away later for wolfhounds for 'roo hunting. While she was still the only one of her kind there Belle romped into a rabbiter's tent one night and in a gregarious fit began to lick the face of the man asleep on the ground. 'My Gawd! I thought it was a damned great wolf slavering over me!' the man screamed. 'I thought I was going to be eaten alive in me bed.'

Few patches of scrub interrupted our view of the encircling horizon dropping over the rim-like edge of the dry saucer on which we lived. Our Welsh stockman friend was following rabbit traps one day and got lost in the sameness of our landscape. The railways sent an engine to run up and down the line blowing its whistle to guide him to the railway. At night he saw the engine headlight and later my mother heard a sound at our door. She opened it and Taffy fell in.

Rain came grudgingly here. Out on the sand where the construction navvies worked boys were employed to run water to the parched men when they called: a sort of Australian version of Gunga Din.

At our railway house at the siding the contents of our two galvanised iron tanks were of such concern and the word 'tank' used so often that babies used the word at an early age. All through summer the clok-clok of knuckles rapping the rims of the tanks could be heard. Dad said that if ever we Smiths had a coat of arms it would be a closed fist raised to rap an iron tank. Everyone as they passed would rap the tanks to see how they were holding. As the dry months rolled by, lower and lower sank the rings that echoed hollowly until there were only a few at the bottom of the tanks that echoed with the weight of water. When we got to this stage we would apply to the Railways Department to send us up a tanker. At times we were down to the last rim before this arrived. Every drop other than for drinking purposes had to be agreed to by Mum. The tap was turned off so tightly that we children couldn't move it, sometimes a padlock was placed on it, and always a tin dish was left on the ground beneath the tap to catch any errant drop that might fall. For ordinary daily ablutions we washed in the tin dish on the tank-stand made of sleepers. In summer we never threw this dish of water out after use in case someone else might want to wash in it. We used fresh water only to wash our faces. On Saturdays we all bathed in the tin bath in the wash-house, heating the water in the wood-fire copper and carrying it in a kerosene tin past the two wash-troughs to the bath. When our tanks were low we all used the same water, Mum first, then we two girls, then Dad. Even then the plug wasn't pulled out. After it had cooled Dad carried the water round to the 'hot-house' under the tank-stand where Mum's plants sulked in this arid air.

But often we were too low in water for the luxury of a bath. Things were like this the day Mum shot at the camel.

Far from shops, we were on the trade route of the Afghan–Indian hawkers, those turbaned traders who brought a colour and *exotique* along with the calico aprons, print dresses, cotton 'bodies', dungaree trousers and 'stuff' for dresses. This was the late 1920s and cars hadn't yet come to the bush in numbers. A moving ball of dust on the horizon announced the coming of the 'Ghan in his horse-drawn wagon. Further out the hawkers used camels, but they only came to our place this once.

Dad was away and Mum was alone. When she saw them coming, the turbaned hawker and his three camels, she knew intuitively what had driven him from his habitual route into strange territory. The drought was everywhere. The railways were so pressed by their commitments to their outback workers that their few tankers could hardly cope with the calls for water. We had waited four weeks. Further west in the wasteland near the South Australian border the position must be desperate.

'Stay inside,' Mum ordered Mick and me. 'Lock the door when I go out.' She took Dad's rifle down from behind the door and loaded it.

The hawker didn't ask for water. He led his animals directly to the tank and put our wash dish under the tap. Inside the house, we girls pressed our faces to the window. Mum rested the rifle across the top of the empty tank. It was a low tank and she stood on the wooden sleepers on which it rested on the ground.

'If you touch that tap,' Mum said, 'I'll shoot your camel.' She sighted along the barrel. I once saw her bring down a crow on the wing. The hawker didn't know this. To him she was a gentle little woman with her protecting man far away.

'My camels must drink, missus,' he said, and turned the tap. As he did, Mum fired. There was the most awesome, reverber- ating explosion and the leading camel fell to the ground. The empty tank had magnified the sound many times and sent it ricocheting round and round the iron cylinder.

'You shoot my camel!' the man screamed.

'I'll shoot you if you don't turn that tap off,' she said, facing the Indian. He turned the tap off.

'I didn't shoot your camel. I fired in front of its nose. A good inch in front.' She was right. The camel had fallen from fright. Weakness had prevented it from bolting. It now lay sulking on the ground, its nose-peg pulled taut by its mates, who desired the wide open spaces, but were held by the leather thongs passed through their nose-pegs.

'I know your animals need water,' Mum said. 'But my children also need water. I will give you water for yourself and tell you where you can get some for your animals.' To the west were Government bores spaced twenty miles or so apart. To the east only twelve miles away was Kulkyne bore.

As they left, swaying slowly in a lumpy line over the plain, Mum stoked the kitchen fire and made herself a cup of tea. Then she began to laugh.

'That jolly tank frightened me nearly as much as it did the camel! I had no idea it would do that. I nearly fell over backwards when it went bang!'

Things were bad that year. One day I saw something strange out on the plain and called, 'Mum, there's something running all over the land.' I thought it was little horses. It was emus, hundreds of them. As though smitten by some agitating disease the usually solitary birds were ranging in a herd. First they would veer one way, then, as a flock of budgerigars do in the air, they would turn and flee in another. The sun burnished their copper-coloured feathers as they ran one way, then as they ran another the sheen dulled. It was egg-laying time and they were looking for the long grasses and scrub patches in which to lay their huge, heavy eggs. During the next few days emu eggs were gathered from a wide area by rabbit-trappers and fettlers and sent down south in boxes. The blacks at Kulkyne ranged widely and brought in enough to keep the station homestead in eggs for the next six months. Mary Woollong, who later died holding the sad title of 'the last of the Kulkyne tribe', turned us from sampling them when she declared, 'I bin eatem six emu egg this

15

breakfast.' Mum knew how to cook with emu eggs by diluting them with water, but she denies ever having used them. Many outback women feared the ridicule of sophisticates over their adaptation and use of natural foods and materials.

Rabbits were easy to catch in the drought. Scratching in the barren, hard-baked earth for roots of grasses no longer growing they became reckless with hunger, and our big wolfhound would be in a quandary which one to grab. Sometimes she'd drop the one she had in her mouth to chase another.

Rabbiting days were usually picnicking days, sometimes with the other fettler and his wife joining us. Mum's food was always the best; Dad was always the most successful rabbiter whether he used traps, gun or dogs. I suppose other children thought the same of their parents, and I suppose we were all right.

ON YOUR BLOCKS

When the rains came they made up for the long dry spell in volume and spontaneity. Shortly before we left Nowingi we were caught in one of these downpours coming home from a sports meeting. Dad was a runner, footballer and axeman. He followed sports meetings around the bush in the way a city man might follow horseraces. This Saturday he had gone up to Carwarp on the goods train in the morning. Mum was to follow in the jinker with us two children after she had attended to the 'down' train.

By the time we trotted into the paddock that had become a sports ground for the day, the Married Ladies' Race was being announced.

'Hold the reins,' Mum told Mick, and she sprang to the

ground. In a few minutes she was racing down the unmarked track, her shoes in one hand, the other holding her hat on her head. Sixteen women were in the race. The men came over from the wood-chopping arena to watch. We could hear Dad shouting, 'Come on, Birdie! You little beauty!' And Mum had won. Then she came back to the jinker, took up the reins and drove over to the post-and-rail enclosure where harness horses could be rested.

'Put your hat straight,' she reprimanded me. 'Wherever will people think we've come from!'

I was very small so I was placed up near the finishing line in the girls' race. That day I laid the pattern I was to follow the rest of my life in such events. Running as I believed with the speed of an arrow I nevertheless watched every other girl in the field pass me, with my sister Mickie's long legs out in front of them all. Some day, I vowed as I wobbled in, last, holding my big hat down with both hands, some day I will win a race.

The big event of the day was the final of the twelve-inch standing block. Dad was there in the arena, spitting on his hands and rubbing them together, gripping his axe handle, balancing it, chalk-marking his log on the places where he would put in strategic blows. There were ten finalists, all well-known axemen of the district. Some had heard the starter count to twenty in their heats before they could put their first blow in. Dad had seen one man get his 'front' in before his own number was called.

Ganger Kelly was there, very much to the fore. He set the logs up on their blocks for the choppers. Now he was talking louder and more Irish than ever he did on weekdays (as Mum said, there wasn't a booth out on the railway track).

'Albert Smith,' he claimed, 'will have turned before half of them have got their first blow in.' We were very proud as we waited on the outskirts of the crowd. Now the starter called for everyone except the choppers to stand away from the blocks.

'Now you choppers listen to me. Face your timber. Listen for your count. If any of you jump the gun you're out. All right!

Step up to your blocks.' One of the choppers began, at the last moment, to dig a foothold in the ground with the heel of his boot. 'You should have thought of that before this, Jack,' the starter called. 'I've got my money on you and by God this isn't good enough!' In time Jack was settled ready so that the starter began again. 'Step up to your wood. Steady. I'm going to begin counting, lads. One . . .' The men looked uninterested, relaxed. 'Two . . .' A man swung his axe back and on the count of three dug it deep into the wood. 'Four . . . five . . .' And as each axeman heard his handicap called, he swung his axe and the blade bit a gash from the log. On droned the starter's voice. 'Six . . . seven . . . eight . . .' and by then eight of the ten men were chopping. 'Nine . . . ten . . . eleven . . . twelve . . . thirteen . . .' Still he counted steadily on while Dad stood waiting to hear his handicap called, cool and unflustered among the volley of sounds from flailing axes and the shouting of the crowd. Slowly he stretched his arm away back and as the starter called 'fifteen' down flashed the blade. The one man left came in on the next count. Now the starter, freed to become a commentator, began describing the event, shouting to make himself heard over the babble of voices and the ringing of the axes. 'And there goes Albert Smith and there goes Dave Harris. There they go! Just watch those boys chop! Champions the ten of them. May the best man win . . . and it better be you, Jack.' Two of the lightly handicapped men had their 'front' in and had turned. Now Dad and the other man off scratch were cutting blow for deep blow. Dave Harris the sleeper-cutter from near the Murray River was first of the scratch-men to turn and Dad was hard on his heels. Kelly was getting more Irish every minute.

'There's me bhoy-o! Cuttin' like the champeen he is an' all. Give it to her, Albert! Hit loike an Irishman!' Mick and I pushed our way to the front of the crowd. The chips were flying. Excited now, the other axemen squatting in the sawdust awaiting the next event were encouraging their mates. Some were calling Dad's name, then more, until it seemed all the world we knew was shouting 'Albert, Albert! Give it to her, Smithy!' Near us squatted a solid man in a singlet with PLUMB AXE branded on it. Through his closed teeth he was rating the blows as they fell, SSSsssSSSsssSSSsss, a sibilant timing that increased evenly, always a little ahead of Dad's blade, SSSsssSSSsssSSSsss, in a contrapuntal beat inciting the axe to pursue, overtake and join the rhythm. But the two wouldn't meet until that mad music was ended – as we watched, the air full of sawdust, dust of the plains, chips and the roar of the tight-packed crowd, we saw Dad's blade slope down almost vertically through the two wedge-shaped cuts on either side of his log and the top rolled slowly off and fell to the ground while the long-drawn-out sigh of the man with PLUMB AXE across his chest fell all the way with it.

Mick and I were pushed aside. Kelly, drunk with pride and a little whisky, charged down through the choppers oblivious of slashing axes whirling round his head. Waving his high black hat over his head he plunged over to Dad and threw his big arms round him. 'I'm proud of you, me bhoy. Have a drink!' He pulled a whisky flask from his pocket, took a swig from it and replaced the bottle unthinkingly.

Dad had won, among other things, a beautiful silver teapot; Mum's prize for the Married Ladies' Race was a silver salt, pepper and mustard set, and my sister had a cake dish. I had, as Dad said, 'what Paddy shot at – nothing.'

That night a cloudburst spilled down on us as we trotted home. Mum put Mick and me on the floor of the jinker and covered us with the 'buggy rug' we always carried. The poor horse, with the drive up in the heat and now the hurrying home because of the rain, broke down and could go no further. Dad had to climb down and lead him home, walking beside him for ten miles in the rain. Up in the jinker Mum held the rug down over us two. Soon we were asleep to the constant jog-jog-jog of the wheels below and the gentle swish of the weather around us. When we reached home Dad lifted us down. Mick and I were bone dry, but poor Mum was wet and cramped in pain from being bent over us so long, and Dad's good navy blue suit was a soggy rag. Next day Mum washed and pressed it and Dad proclaimed that it was as good as new. As for the weather, it was forgotten. All we remembered was the great day we'd had at the sports.

'We Smiths certainly scooped the pool!' Dad crowed.

ON THE
WALLABY

B y the time I was five years old we began moving in earnest.
For the rest of our childhood we were never in one place
longer than two years. Often our stay was only for a few
months.

'We mightn't have much money but we can have a lot of
fun,' Dad contended.

Moving was fun. There was the packing, the arrival at the
siding of the trucks that would take our goods, the preparation
of cages for our chooks to travel in, coaxing the cow into the
cattle truck, and Billy our white horse into the loose-box truck
and lashing the jinker onto a flat-top, locking the white cockatoo
into a cage where he protested non-stop at the indignity, getting
the Major Mitchell cockatoo into a box so we could carry her

with us – 'Poor little Chew-Chew can't travel alone' – and then getting the dog to the guard's van, where she lay with her head on her paws and moaned with loneliness until we released her at the end of the journey. Mum would be days getting ready. When we left Nowingi her great difficulty was to keep things clean as she packed them. As fast as she washed the glass of picture frames and the 'good' crockery the dust would swirl in and film it over again.

She packed well. She was a great knick-knack collector and our lounge had up to seventy bits of knick-knackery on the mantelpiece, sideboard and wherever else it could be crowded. Thirty-five pictures in glass-fronted frames hung on the walls. Her great boast in later years was that on all her many moves she never broke one article.

On the day we were to move from Nowingi the ganger and the fettlers came to help pack the furniture and boxes of small things on the railway trucks. Mick and I watched our chance, and when their backs were turned we pushed our own valuables in where they wouldn't be noticed until the truck was unpacked at the other end – 'spare' dolls' legs, bits of broken toys, wheels off old prams; almost everything Mum sent us to convey to the rubbish tip we managed to get unnoticed into the truck.

Then the house was empty. We walked forlornly round the box-like rooms. Suddenly the adventure was spiritless, dead, undesired. We were leaving this place that had sheltered us. Of a sudden we were without a home, bereft of friends; these people we had known were already left vaguely behind us. We knew no one where we were going. The windows were bare and I could see out across the plains where the emus had run like little horses, and the tanks where the camels had come in to drink in the drought. Far up the Mallee the engine whistled to warn of its approach.

'Well,' said Kelly the ganger, 'you haven't left anything you value, have you?'

'Yes,' said the usually undemonstrative Mum. 'We are leaving a friend.' The old man was embarrassed and took his hat off and turned it over in his hands. Mickie spoke up as only a child can.

'Is that the same hat? Dad says it is.'

'It is, Kathleen Mavourneen. I've never had another. It's a good hat.'

'It is a good hat,' said Mum. 'A shady hat.' And we all went out to meet the train.

Ours was a second-class pass, but we travelled like aristocrats because everyone knew we were railway people. Sometimes on the long journey down to Spencer Street, which was the end of the line for most country trains, the guard would sit with us in between stations, and everyone else in the carriage was an outsider as we talked of stations and lines and fettlers and Casey Joneses and told jokes about the 'heads'. Once the engine-driver in his faded blue cloth cap and overalls with a sweat-rag round his neck came in to say good day to Dad while the engine was taking on water. There wasn't a child on the train that didn't envy us then. One little boy wearing Police and Firemen braces over his shirt stood at our door and gaped and didn't move until the driver left.

Swiftly we got to know Victoria. It seemed we chose all the places with the most outlandish names: Quambatook, Warragul, Drouin, Bunyip, Briagalong, Wingeel, Minyip.

'Where are you going?' friends would ask us. When we'd tell them they'd reply, 'Never heard of it.' We wouldn't be surprised. We usually hadn't heard of it either until Mum and Dad would see it in the *Railway Gazette* as COMING VACANT. Our *Gazette* was always well handled. In these circulars were advertised transfers as well as vacancies for fettlers, station-masters and station-mistresses, gangers, etc. What we looked for were those which advertised for fettler and wife, the woman to be caretaker at the station. Mum had passed the necessary examinations for this position. When they saw a place advertised the school atlas was brought out and we'd try to run it to earth. More often than not the town itself would not be marked, being, as Dad described such towns, 'a one-horse outfit', but some large town nearby would give a rough clue as to its whereabouts.

Waaia was not on any map. We had to go there before we knew where it was. We didn't even know how to pronounce it. The day we arrived the station phone rang. Mum answered and said, 'Mrs Smith speaking.'

The caller asked, 'What station is that?'

'I can't tell you,' answered the new station-mistress. 'I can spell it but I can't say it.' (It is pronounced Way-eye.)

Here life became a settled thing. We stayed for two years in Waaia, then moved away for eighteen months and back again for another two years, so it was the place where we spent more of our lives than anywhere else.

Waaia was north of Shepparton in the Goulburn Valley. For most of the year there was not much rail traffic. On the five weekdays the 'Beetle' came through, an old bus-shaped, petrol-consuming passenger coach on rail wheels painted black and yellow in stripes. This brought our mail and daily paper and arrived at 2 p.m., went to the end of the line at Picola, turned, and passed Waaia on the way back towards Melbourne at 4 p.m. Once a week a steam engine hauled a goods train through. This was during the winter and early spring; but come mid-summer and Waaia station really hummed! The tiny one-pub, one-store town was in the centre of a wheat-growing area and was the dispatch station for hundreds of thousands of bushels of wheat each year. Those days Mum would go up to the little station building at 8 a.m. and might not be able to come back down to the house until 6 p.m. Somehow, in between all this she still managed to continue turning out the meals for us that made us the best-fed children in the district. Apart from allotting trucks and departure dates she had to direct where the wheat stacks should be erected in the station grounds. Each buyer had his own stacks. There was a huge wheat shed at the far end of the station yard for 'holding' bags of grain – in those days there were no silos in that area – but the great bulk of wheat was in stacks in the yard.

At 6 p.m. the big gates into the railway yard were closed and padlocked for the night. Each morning at 8 a.m. they were unlocked. In the busy part of the year this became my job. The first morning I did this I thought nothing more wonderful could happen to me in my life, and now, many years later, I'm not sure I wasn't right.

While Mum went up to the station and began sorting out her way-bills and adjusting the date stamp I went skip-hopping down between the rails, jumping from sleeper to sleeper to where the wagons waited with their loads outside the gate. Already the sun was hot, glaring down from a cloudless blue sky, reflecting back from the golden, dusty land. As far as could be seen along the dirt road wagons were lined up. There were a few trucks, but mostly they were horse-drawn wagons. The drivers squatted in the shade of the wheels yarning, chewing wheat stalks to keep them off the cigarettes. It was not yet 8. Swinging the big keys in my hand I stepped over the cattle grid at the crossing and walked on to the road and looked down the long line of wagons. Some horses snuffled into their nosebags; others, unhitched, were being led up to the water trough for a drink – a man wouldn't move his wagon away from the gate: if he lost his place in the queue it could easily wreck his chance of getting a second and perhaps even a third load in that day before the gate closed at night. It was preferable to go through the tedious process of unhitching the team and leading them back to water. Young Roy Tweddle, who was only fifteen years old, was coming down the road with four horses so unhitched. His father had one of the best properties in the wheat belt and if his wagon wasn't first in line of a morning it was never further back than second or third.

Across the road opposite the gate stood the Waaia Hotel. It was strategically placed, for the heat and the dust and the long wait in the queue all through the day for a place on the weighbridge made a man thirsty. On a long stool on the verandah sat Yorky, the hotel 'boots'. He would sit there all day, only going inside for meals. It was said of him that the most useful thing he did for his keep was to whistle, a thing he did exquisitely. On his breast, its faded ribbon now almost colourless, he wore the Khedive Star with three bars. He told me he had been up the Nile in the epic venture to relieve Gordon besieged in Khartoum. Now he spent his days watching the wagons roll by, taking a beer when it was offered him, and whistling, always whistling. He never ceased.

As the big gate swung open the lead wagon rolled forward. Behind it, Roy Tweddle called 'Hup!' and the call was taken up man after man back along the road – 'Hup!' – and the day had begun.

I hooked the gate back to its fastening post and stood on the lower rung and watched them roll by, the smell of the golden, warm grain settling all round me. As the wagons hesitated on the weighbridge the buyers went along and stabbed long brass sample tubes into the bags to test for quality. Farther up the yard the lumpers were trailing across to the stacks. Chella Valenti the Italian was already there starting up the motor on an elevator. Big Bill Martin roared past me on his motor-bike. These were big men and strong. Bill Martin could carry three bags at a time on his motor-bike for a stunt, one across his shoulders, one in front of him and one on the handle-bars.

Dad and the gang were going by on the rail tracks on the Casey Jones. Here in summer the great danger was fire while the wheat crops were huge, tall, dry tinder-beds. Wheat then was much taller than today's compact crop. A spark from an engine, a carelessly thrown cigarette butt, even a piece of glass could start a holocaust that would engulf the whole district. Each morning the gang patrolled the whole length of their section till they met up with the gang at the end of the next section south. Now as they went the long sticks of their fire-beaters stuck out behind the motor. Dad saw me and gave his usual thumb-in-the-air wave.

Back at the house Mickie had let the chooks out and now they scattered across the line to feed on the free wheat about the stacks. Slowly I walked home. At the first stack wheat was already going up the elevator to the lumpers. Their dress was uniform; sandshoes slit open at the sides for ventilation and to allow the wheat to slip out, dungaree trousers, bare chest with head and shoulders covered by a sack turned hood-shaped to protect the skin from the sandpaper-like bags of grain. To leave all this and sit in school! I thought of wagging it as Mickie occasionally did, but I didn't have the courage.

THE
BEST YEARS

No matter how often we had to go to a new school, that first day was always frightening. We were on guard. We had both already been to several schools and knew we had to be ready for almost anything. At Waaia we got on better than anywhere else. When the twenty-odd pupils had marched in and sat down the teacher sized Mickie and me up where we stood by his desk holding our slates and lunch bags. We, in turn, sized him up. Would he be a shouter, a strap man, a kind but useless teacher, a martinet, a weeper? We had had them all. Schoolmasters at an early age – this one was twenty years old – they must teach eight grades, with an average of six subjects to each class, with no one to refer to should they strike trouble. This responsibility developed big personalities or worried them to uselessness.

This man didn't hurry us, he let us take our time. After a while we were satisfied and returned his grin.

'Are you any good at anything?' he asked Mick. Honest Mick said, no, she wasn't.

'Oh well,' he said. 'No good worrying about something we can't mend.' Mickie grinned from ear to ear. They were friends.

I was in the third grade. Moving from school to school did not trouble me as it did some children; instead, the different methods of teaching seemed to me to stimulate application. The only drawback to being two grades ahead of others of my age was that I was associated with children of a greater age emotionally than mine – to say nothing of size. There were two others in grade three. Boys. Ted Jorgenson and Alan Thornton. We sat in a long desk that held six children. To my right were two grade-two kids, to my left the two grade-three boys and beside them a lone grade-four girl, a big girl who had been in grade four for two years and was already fourteen years old and technically able to leave school.

I hated those long seats. For one thing you couldn't spread; for another, sitting with children bigger than yourself you were apt to get 'the treatment'. At playtime this first day at Waaia the boys on either side of me played an old trick. Instead of filing out they stayed seated, pretending to be busy with their slates. I therefore couldn't get out. I attempted to stand up to climb over the back of the seat and found I was anchored by my long curls to the back-rest. It is very difficult to undo your hair from that position. The teacher had seen none of this, or so I thought. He was busy at the blackboard with his back to us. I looked up, thinking to call out to him, and while I looked his arm came out behind him and picked up a ruler from his desk. As he turned he aimed it straight at Ted Jorgenson's head, from which it bounced and hit the floor. To Pete Marvel on the other side of me he said, 'You'll get the inkwell if you don't move quick.'

The school was next to the Waaia recreation ground, a great

paddock containing a fine football field, cricket oval, two tennis courts, a basketball court and a rounders field. There was vigour in the little one-pub, one-store town. We could use all these playing fields; indeed a wooden stile was built over the school fence to make access easier. As well, our own school ground was a quarter of a mile long and had basketball and tennis courts. Though I was useless at all sports this extravagant abundance didn't upset me. After all, one has to be bad not to gain a place in a team where there are only nineteen children in the school. Using every girl we had we still must impress boys to get a basketball team and opposition. And in turn, the boys press-ganged us girls in eight-a-side football and cricket. My sister Mickie was one of the best footballers in the school.

There was an old, gnarled pepper-corn tree in the grounds. All pepper-corn trees are easy to climb, having natural footholds in the trunks, and very sit-onable branches, but this was the most inviting I ever saw. A girl could sit there half the day reading if she got on the right side of the teacher and finished her work early. I was not allowed to read at home so had to think of ruses whereby I could read at school. I decided to start right away. Among the four books in the cupboard in the school was *Peter Pan and Wendy*. When I'd completed the next lesson I held my slate over the book and began to read. I'd never read anything like it! It was wonderful! But Ted Jorgenson kept disturbing me, fidgeting and spreading his elbows as he picked at a capsule in the palm of his hand with his pen nib. When I retaliated by elbowing him he jabbed me with the pen. Then he took out a pocketknife and began prying into the capsule with that. Now I didn't like to prod him, he might just as quickly give me a touch with the point of the knife.

I decided to take my book out to the tree. I stood up to ask permission to leave the room and slid out the end of the seat. The kids who had let me out still hadn't had time to slide back in when there was a loud explosion behind us, and turning back I saw Ted Jorgenson looking in bewilderment at his hand where three severed fingers hung down and blood ran in a pool on the

31

desk. Pieces of the casing of the detonator lay on the seat where they had fallen. My slate was shattered on the desk.

The young teacher came calmly across the room and held his arm round the boy. 'Maisie,' he said to the grade-four girl I had thought not so bright. 'Get the first-aid kit and stay behind to help me. Alex, harness your horse and bring your cart round to the door. The rest of you get your hats and go home.'

I went straight home, carefully by-passing the station where I could see Mum busy behind the counter. She would not expect me until 4 p.m., and the return of the 'Beetle' at that time would warn me.

There was nowhere in the house to hide a book. I went round to the wash-house where the copper and the bath and wash-troughs were, but Mick was there hiding some *Peg's Papers* she had swapped at school. She was always getting caught with *Peg's Paper, True Confessions* and the like, so I knew that this was not a safe place. There was only one place left, so I went down the yard, closed the door and sat down and sped so far away with the Darling family that I didn't hear the train come or go, nothing at all, until my mother called me. Then I hid the book in the place I'd decided on and went out. Mick was emerging from the wash-house. Mum was very suspicious. Late that afternoon before the sun set Mum suddenly screamed from the back yard. We ran out to see her backing out from the lavatory. I felt sick. She must have found it. She would take it away. Oh no, no, no, don't make me have to swear not to read it again. I'd sworn before on the cross on the rosary beads, and when I did I'd never go back on whatever I'd promised. I never felt faint with distress. Instead, my inside seemed to turn purple like the mouth of a blue-tongued lizard. I wouldn't swear! No one would take that book. I raged down the yard.

Mum heard me coming. 'Stand back,' she called. 'It's coming out now.' Her arm swung back then down, *thwack*! swishing the piece of fencing wire she held down on the back of the brown snake that had been in the outhouse. Dad was coming through the gate on his way home from work and she carried the snake on a stick up to show him. I ran in and put my hand down the lining that came only halfway up the lavatory wall. There it was, safe and untouched. I sat on the seat in pleasure and excitement to rest, just holding the book in my hand. Next thing I knew there was a commotion outside. Where was I?

'Here,' I called.

'Oh dear God, what will she do next? Come out before you're bitten to death!'

Carefully I replaced the book down the lining and went out to where they waited for me in exasperation. To calm the air Dad asked me how I got on at school.

'I'm about third in my class at the moment.'

'How many in the class?'

'Three.'

'Splendid!' he said. 'You've only got to beat two more and you'll be dux.' The self-confidence of country children is rarely shaken; the competition is never such as to make them know failure.

WE WERE 'PATS'

G oing to church was as much a social event as a religious
experience in the bush. There were few other places to
which one could wear a pretty hat and a frilly dress.
There was no Catholic church at Waaia. Ten miles down the
line at Numurkah there was one and ten miles up the line at
Nathalia was another, so church-going there was a sort of safari.

Because it was not a simple matter for us to attend church we
never took the services lightly, as one grown too familiar with
them may. Each contact claimed our devout and painstaking
attention, as the priest found out when I made my first communion.

'How have you sinned against Almighty God?' he asked me
after I'd given the ritual appeal of 'Bless me, father, for I have
sinned.'

Without hesitating I told him, 'I say bloody. Sometimes I'm worse and I say . . .' His alacrity in preventing my revealing further the crimes that I had spent many hours spread over many weeks investigating and collating was disappointing. I was afraid I had misunderstood him.

'When I'm mad I call my mother . . .'

Again he leapt in.

'No doubt she gives you a certain penance at the time,' he said, dryly. (I didn't tell him, but I would automatically put my hand out for the razor strop each time I let drop a 'silencer', as Dad called these words.)

I said my penance and left the church. I had had the priest's blessing. Oh the joy of a clean sheet, the stainless soul, and then a kid I hated, Paul Amery, clouted me over the side of the head as he ran by and I yelled out, 'You b . . .' and suddenly it dawned on me: today was only Friday and I had to last until Sunday when I would make my first communion in the state of grace. If I said b . . . even once I'd not be able to go to communion and everyone would know that the only reason for me to miss would be that I had sinned. And so began the long vigil. The great Australian adjective proved itself capable of being used as a noun, verb, conjunction, adverb, a whole sentence. By the time Sunday morning dawned I felt I was running one jump only ahead of the devil himself. Then they lowered the veil over my eyes, rose petals fluttered from the baskets for us small children to tread upon as we came two by two down the aisle, and our parents prayed and the organ played and the voices called, 'O Mary, we crown thee with blossoms today, Queen of the Angels, Queen of the May.' I knew I had the best dress of all, white silk. 'Suffer the little children to come unto me,' recited the priest. And afterwards there were cream cakes and raspberry cordials that left red moustaches round our mouths, and women treating us with such deference as we'd never seen before. Then we floated home.

There was only one other Catholic family at Waaia, the Youngs. The father was a wheat-buyer, the mother a London-trained dressmaker; their son Kevin was my age. Inevitably our two families became friends. Kevin shared the only real friendship I had during my childhood. I feel that the reason neither my sister nor I could have friends has no place in this book or on my tongue. She and I talk about it sometimes now, mostly in complaint to one another that we have too many friends and not enough time to ourselves. When we were young we were bitter. Now we are grown women with children of our own, with heart-hurts and disappointments already behind us like skins we have had to slough off to gain stability.

I was lucky to be able to have Kevin. I was seven years old when I went to Waaia. He and I were friends until we were adults and he died. We were both musical, and what was termed 'quick' at school. We planned there at Waaia what we would do with our lives. I wrote then, I would always write. He would become a doctor. And so it came to pass. We talked out our plans there beside the wheat stacks long before we told anyone else. Such aspirations, we knew, would be considered freakish in our circumstances. When Kevin died, only three years after taking his degree and setting up in practice, the cool, clear candlelight of childhood was extinguished.

The Youngs were English and their outlook on going to church was different from ours. Some people said we were 'bog Irish'. Be that as it may, I never met a non-Irish priest until I was fifteen years old, and then he came from Irish parents. The Youngs had two cars. On occasions they would drive in to church, but only if it were convenient. The ten-mile drive was over a dusty, bumpy, potholed road and they felt it was unreasonable for one to travel weekly on such a road. We were horrified. Miss Mass because the road was bad? Why, Mum drove the jinker drawn by Billy our grey harness pony many Sundays over the same bumpy ten miles of red road. Occasionally, though he was not a Catholic, Dad took us in on the Casey Jones.

One Sunday morning Mum sent me to ask if the Youngs were going to drive in. No, they told me, they couldn't, they had guests. From where I stood in the vestibule I could see the visitors sipping tea. I knew these people must hear everything I said, but it made no difference to one brought up as I had been.

'That's a mortal sin', I said, 'to miss Mass on Sundays.'

Mrs Young looked startled. 'Now, now,' she said.

I replied, 'You'll burn in hellfire everlasting.' She evidently thought the heat had affected me, for she gave me a drink of cordial from the Coolgardie safe. It did cool me down. I think I had a second one. By the time I arrived home it was too late for Billy to be driven the ten miles in by road. So Mum drove him up the railway track, which was nearly two miles shorter.

With Mick and me hanging on beside her she drove on the narrow cleared fire-break beside the fence. Where roads cut the line and post-and-rail fences blocked our path we'd let the sliprails down and drive Billy over. Sometimes there were ditches. Then we'd all get out and walk, Mum leading Billy by the reins close up to his mouth. The jinker wheels would grip in the dry drainage gully and Mum would urge the pony on, clicking her tongue, coaxing him gently, scolding and threatening him with the whip. And then we'd be over, the sliprails up again, and off we'd go at a grand old bat to make up for time lost. There were dry boughs that had broken off trees during thunderstorms across the track, and Mick would clamber off the iron step and drag these aside; there were other living boughs hanging low from trees and we'd all duck, Mum holding our heads down with her arm. Then we were on the outskirts of Numurkah and able to get out onto the main road cum street.

Mum immediately looked us over. 'Look at your hair,' she warned me. I twisted the curls round my finger. 'Kathleen! What have you got on your face!' Mick spat on her handkerchief and rubbed vigorously at odd spots. 'And the pair of you, look at your socks!' Mum despaired of raising two little ladies. We hitched our stockings up and folded them over our garters. Shoe-dusting was easy. We both wore black stockings, so dragged our shoes over the backs of our legs when Mum wasn't looking. She was straightening her own hat and pulling on her gloves. Billy was given a drink and secured to the hitching post outside the church. There was only one other horse there but several motor-cars. Mum lined us up one on either side of her and ran her eye over us. Evidently satisfied, she led the way in, the three of us holding our handbags in our left hands, prayer books in our right. No one could call us bush bumpkins!

Once a month a priest came from Nathalia to a little bush church five miles south-west of us. If we walked to the turn-off a mile and a half from Waaia he would pick us up and drive us the rest of the way in his car. I liked this church best of all. It was the only actual 'bush' church I ever went to. Because Mass must be celebrated by a priest Catholics have not tended to build the little chapel in the bush that so many Churches served by lay preachers have done. It was a square room in the middle of the golden land. It held about twenty people. There were a few long, backless stools, but for the most part we sat on strong boards resting on boxes for support. The first time I went there I knelt on the floor to say my prayers then sat back – right on the head of a man who was leaning on the seat praying. For a terrible moment as he lifted his head I rose in the air, then Mum pulled my arm and I bumped off.

There was no vestry there to which the priest could retire to don his vestments, so he had to robe and disrobe in front of the congregation. Instead of the procession to the altar warning you that Mass was about to begin, he'd say, '*Nomine Patris et Filius . . .*' and there'd be people sitting, standing, walking round and talking. But there was a quality of feeling there I never knew in any other church. We'd all of us come from scattered places in a ten-mile radius to this lonely building to take part in this strange, beautiful, mystical ceremony. There we shared the simplicity, the belief, the hope, the prayers and the company of people like ourselves.

Because of the lack of a vestry the end of Mass was as peremptory as the beginning. One Sunday Father Healy gave the blessing, old Jack Heggarty who was acting as altar 'boy' said,

'Amen', and the priest turned and in his thick brogue said, 'And phwat d'ye think is goin' to win the Cup, Jack?'

The same old Irish priest forgot us one day. It was so hot that a mirage crept ahead of us all the way to the turn-off. We were stretched back along the road in a tired line, our shoulders hunched and heads down under the heat and glare. For an hour we sat on the fence posts at the turn-off, but he didn't come, so we had to walk home again. We were all fasting from midnight the night before in anticipation of going to communion. We would have borne it stoically had it not been for the embarrassment of having Ted O'Grady with us. Ted had worked at the store at Waaia for a year and never been to church. With a name like O'Grady he must be a 'Pat', Mum reasoned, so of course he must be gathered in.

'I'll go just this once,' the wicked young man said, and once only it was.

Nowadays one need not fast before going to communion. In those days not even a sip of water was permitted from midnight until after the sacrament was administered. Terrible? No. Not a one of us – except Ted O'Grady – begrudged our good intention as we came light-headedly, head-achingly up the track to home that day. (Mass then could only be celebrated between midnight and midday.)

After Mass at this bush church the priest would have a cup of tea from the thermos one of the women would bring for him, and the men would squat on their heels under the solitary gum outside and chew a piece of bark just as did the men in John O'Brien's poem, and just like the men in that poem they talked about the crops, and the rain that was always too late or too early or not there at all. And the women would have an impromptu meeting to decide who would launder the altar cloths next, and we kids would charge round playing 'He' and all of us would forget we hadn't eaten or drunk since the day before. Then we'd drive off, some in gigs, some on horses and some in cars.

SITTING
LOOSELY IN
THE SADDLE

There was a boy from the city whose name was Marcus Fox came to stay with the Youngs in 1934. He was not a remarkable boy, but I never forgot him. He was the first child I ever heard say he couldn't find anything to do.

Mrs Young and Mum spoke about it. 'He might be homesick,' Mum pondered.

Mrs Young had a different theory. 'I don't think he's a very bright boy.'

We always had something to do. The great difficulty was to keep hidden from our parents many of the things we did do. Such as horse-riding or, to quote Adam Lindsay Gordon, 'sitting loosely in the saddle' – if, of course, we had had a saddle! We didn't own a riding hack, but there was never a time in our lives when we couldn't ride. We always had a jinker or gig and from the time I was a baby Dad would sit me on the back of the harness horse as he brought it in to harness up. There are pictures at home of Mick and me on horses from the time we were toddlers onwards. Always bareback and always in dresses. Quite a few kids rode to school. They rode bareback on a bag or folded rug, the boys in short trousers and sandshoes, the girls in ordinary cotton dresses. Hunting pink, riding breeches and black velvet caps were unknown amongst the real horsemen and women of the Australian bush. There can be no more inspiring equestrian sight than a bush girl with her hair flying out behind her, her dress tucked in under her knees in front and fluttering out at the back, and yelling out, 'Hey! Watch me!' as she and the horse take a fallen log together.

Mickie was a good rider. She had that dare-devilry that horses sense and respond to. A horse that jog-trotted for me would break into a gay gallop for her. On weekdays we'd ride the horses at school owned by other children; on Saturday we usually managed to ride our own harness horse. Dad coached a football team at Nathalia and he and Mum would set off before lunch on the little inspection motor along the line and wouldn't return until tea-time. We'd continue industriously with our washing-up or bed-making until the sound of the motor disappeared. Then we were off.

Billy was the best of all the horses that came and went in our house paddock. He could usually be trusted outside the fence. The others, used only to harness, would go crazy when we got on their back and would have taken the bit between their teeth and headed for the scrub if we'd let them out the sliprails. One such horse nearly killed Mickie one day. It shivered and whinnied while we struggled to put the bridle on and throw a bag over its back, but stood quite still when Mick climbed on while I held its head. The tensions bottled up inside showed only in its rolling eyes and flat ears.

'He'll get used to me,' Mick called. Off she went to the far end of the paddock and around the solitary ghost gum, the horse

41

pig-rooting all the way. As she turned she dug her heels in and off he went in a long, even stride. Mick's hair was flying out red-gold behind her, her skirt flowed back over his rump, her long legs crouched round him. Near the rails she hauled him back on his haunches.

'Open them up, I'm going out,' she ordered. I hesitated.

'Open them or I'll jump them,' she said. She pulled on the bridle and said, 'Back boy, back,' and the horse backed with a pushing movement as he was used to doing in the jinker. Mick tucked her legs up so her knees would take the weight off the horse when he jumped and gathered the reins in. She would jump all right! I let the rails down. 'Yahoo!' Mickie shouted. The horse lit off like a rocket out into the railway yards down the track. Mick was laughing, the horse's hooves thudded on the hard earth, then it veered off the track and across the rails. Mick couldn't drag its head round and it ran beneath a thick bough of a gum which caught her sideways across the head and flung her to the ground. When I got to her she was lying on her back with her eyes closed. I looked at her. 'What's the matter?' She didn't say anything. 'Why don't you get up?' Still she was silent. I thought she was pretending to be asleep so I went home and left her there. It was nearly dark when she came in. She had a drink of water at the tap and then began to retch.

Before Mum returned we had coaxed the horse back into the house paddock with dry feed and had taken the bridle off. We explained away the lather of sweat by saying we thought it had seen a snake, because it had been bolting round the paddock all afternoon in fear.

This same thick bough unseated Mick another time, but then it was with the better-behaved Billy and was Mick's own fault. She rode him hell for leather down to the gates one Saturday and called back, 'How's that?' Then, 'I'll show you a trick.' She swivelled round on his broad white back and faced back to front. Taking the reins in her hands behind her back she shouted, 'Yahoo!' and kicked out, her heels drumming into the animal's ribs. He shot off like a streak of lightning. Mick as usual was laughing and calling out. Suddenly the hard hoof-beats thudded more softly. Billy, guided by the reins Mick held without being able to see her path, obediently swung off the track, straight towards the gum. Down went Mickie again, the bough catching her across the back of the head. She was sicker still this time, and all I did was kneel over her begging her to open her eyes and crying. She was a quiet girl for a few days after that.

Billy not only was a good horse to ride, he looked wonderful. An all-white, he paced like a racer and kept his neck arched high. Both on together Mick and I would jog down to the railway gates, open them up, then off up the road we'd gallop, me holding loosely onto Mick's waist, my head turned sideways to miss her flying hair.

Usually we rode over to Marvels' place, probably because that was the last place Mum would have let us go had she known it well. As it was, her social contact with the Marvels was limited to an invitation she had accepted from Mr Marvel for herself and Dad to go there to play cribbage one night, and then she saw no further than the living-room.

'I feel Mrs Marvel hadn't quite expected us,' Mum said.

Mrs Marvel not only expected her but went further than I ever saw her go again by shifting the cats, dogs and poultry out and removing the traces of their shortcomings. She was the dirtiest woman I ever knew. Her husband, 'Bull' Marvel, ran trotters. His son Pete, who was only my age, exercised them; you could hear him trotting them round and round the paddock when you lay warm in bed on cold winter mornings. Their house had probably been a fine home once. The kitchen had a flagged floor and great iron fittings over the iron range, heavy oak furniture and beams across the ceiling. As well as a lounge room there was a parlour with crumbling antimacassars on crumbling chairs, and a crumbling green plush cover over the now tinny piano. There were two pictures on the wall and faded patches showed where others had hung. 'When Dad makes me get morning sticks I cut up anything I can find,' Pete told us, indicating that the remaining frames wouldn't be there much longer.

In contrast to the excess of 'living' rooms there were only two bedrooms. The Marvel family numbered twelve. Opposite the parlour the parents slept in one small bedroom. Under a horse rug at the end of the double bed, Pete slept. He was one of the toughest, most unlovable children ever born, but when he died under that horse rug on that horrid bed at the age of eight we cried for him.

The other bedroom was tiny too, and in the double bed that filled it almost wall to wall slept the two eldest sons. The rest of the family used the front verandah where a piece of sacking formed a 'sun-blind' across the front, and there, underneath two bags in two double beds, slept the rest of the brood. Mum taught us nothing about the facts of life. The Marvels left nothing to our imagination. We knew that if Mum knew this and knew that we went there, there would be the dickens to pay, but the place had that carelessness that is a lure for children who come from homes where discipline is strict. If we sneaked out to the home of anyone else in the district we would be asked, 'Does your mother know you're here?' and our parents would be told of the visit. The Marvels worked on the reverse pattern. They would teach us how to avoid detection.

They owned several hundred acres of land, a little of which was sown in wheat by a neighbour who leased a patch, but the rest was untended, as they were too indolent to do anything about it. There was old machinery lying everywhere. Reapers, binders, harrows, ploughs, and threshing machines stood in paddocks like memorials to lost enthusiasm. In the big machinery shed harness mouldered and grew fur; horse collars hung from nails, their stuffing poking out where rats made nests; old wheels and a broken sulky tangled in a corner; and what must have been one of the first cars brought to that district was used as a roost by hens. In a pile of decayed horse rugs and driving gear on the floor a fox once hid her cubs and when one of the boys found them they had been there so long they were big enough to run away and escape.

44

We never knew if the cow-shed had been abandoned because it was falling apart or if it was falling apart because it had been abandoned. It is likely that the latter was the case because the cows were now milked on the house verandah, which was certainly more convenient.

There was never a dull moment at Marvels'. One Saturday when Mum and Dad were away we rode over and played football with them. The ball they had was like a big milk-coloured balloon. It had a cord at one end and this was fastened shut with cat-gut.

'That's the pig's bladder,' Pete told us. 'That pipe's where he . . .'

On the ride home Mick warned me, 'Don't tell Mum!'

Yabbying in their dam was fun. It was a big dam, full of bright, rust-coloured water surrounded by rust-coloured soil banks. We'd bait our pieces of string with pieces of raw meat and lower them under the surface. When the yabbies took the bait we'd haul in slowly until their 'whiskers' were just out of the water then scoop them up quickly with a net we made of chicken wire fastened to a piece of fencing wire. Young Pete, the boy who trained the trotters, could get the little grey yabbies out by hand; he was an excellent bush boy. But he was also a cruel boy. He claimed that 'spraggies' (sparrows) were the best bait and he'd pull young naked birds out of nests and tear them apart while they were alive and tie the still flinching pieces to the string. I hated him. If you were taking a short cut home across the paddock when he was training the trotters he'd ride straight at you to see you run for the fence.

Then, one morning, he didn't take the horses out. He had rheumatic fever. He never rode again.

'He's been crook like this before,' old Marvel told Dad. 'He complained all last week. But he rode all right. Treated the horses well.'

Mrs Young and Mum went across to see him and found him huddled under the horse rug at the end of the double bed in his work shirt and socks. Mrs Young made a red flannel night-shirt and took bottles of warm broth to him. He died early one morning and the parents found him at lunchtime. Next day the Marvel kids turned up at school.

'You could have stayed home,' the teacher told them.

Their answer made some of us weep, not for them, but for poor unloved Pete: 'We haven't missed a day yet,' they said. The teacher sent us all home in the afternoon in memory of Pete, whose last atonement was still on the blackboard, 'I must not stick pens in the ceiling', one hundred times. He had only got to forty-nine times on the Friday before he died. There were still some of the nibs in the ceiling above our heads that the broom hadn't been able to dislodge.

Mum and Mrs Young went across and offered to lay him out. Mum took one of my plain white cotton singlets, a pair of white socks and a white linen sheet. They washed him and dressed him in the socks and singlet and the red flannel night-shirt and wrapped the sheet about him. That afternoon Mr Marvel drove into Numurkah to the undertaker with the little boy, now wrapped in the horse rug, and left him at the makeshift morgue. He brought the sheet across to Mum that night.

'You don't want to go losing a good sheet, missus,' he said. Mum told him we would all be going in to the funeral, but he told us we were too late.

'They were going to get on with it when I left.'

Dad asked, 'Weren't you wanting to see the little chap to the end of the road, Syd?' But he said no, there was no use crying over spilt milk.

In our house we cried often over that little boy as he lay lonely in death and we listened to the thud of the horses' hooves beating by each dawn as someone else exercised the trotters.

9

THEY'RE OFF

T he bookmakers shouted the odds, the horses were lined up at the barrier, the starters looked to their timepieces, and Waaia races were off to a flying start.

The racecourse was Ernie Brenzing's paddock two miles out of town. For days beforehand women had been cooking. Our wood-fuel copper had bubbled all one day with Christmas puddings and all the next with hams. The kitchen table was a litter of flour, icing sugar, eggs, cream, sandwich fillings, sweets to be sold in baskets, and vegetable salads. There was so much of everything that it spilled over to the table on the back verandah and the table in the lounge. The suite in the lounge – we called it the 'front room' in those days – was out of sight beneath boxes of sponges, brandy snaps, cream puffs and pastry boats. Mick and I poked our fingers into everything when we could get away from the everlasting washing-up. We were still on holidays after Christmas. It was mid-summer and the heat was terrific. The wood stove kept the temperature in the kitchen well above the century. At midday we took the dishes out to the tank-stand and went on washing up there away from the enclosed heat, but Mum must bear with it till the end of the day. She was cooking for the luncheon booth.

Dad had taken the afternoon off from work to help erect the judge's box (a hessian shade over his head) and mend the railings round the course and put up the tents and marquees for the serving of meals, and for the 'refreshment booth' as well as the hessian-encircled lavatories which he called the 'Houses of Parliament'.

That night we children were ordered to bathe in the tin bath out in the wash-house, a thing we normally did only on Saturdays, and told to say our prayers quickly and get into bed. For Mum to tell us to say prayers 'quickly' meant that she was very busy indeed. We were scarcely in bed when she hauled us out again. I was to try on a new dress she was making for me, Mick was to put her 'good' dress on to see if it fitted. Mine satisfied Mum, a few tucks here and there and it would be finished. Then she turned to Mick.

'Oh no! Oh dear God! Kathleen! Pull it down! You couldn't have grown that much!' Mum tugged at the dress. 'When did you have it on last?'

Dad came to the door to see what the hullabaloo was about. Then he saw Mick. He laughed. 'Whacko!' said Dad. 'Roll 'em, girls, roll 'em, and show the boys your knees.'

'Albert!' Mum exclaimed, shocked.

'There's nothing wrong with that song,' Dad said. 'Everyone was singing it when we first met and all the girls were rolling their stockings down and showing as much leg as Mickie . . .'

'That was different.' Mum had the last word. Dad took one final look at Mick's long, coltish legs sticking down from this high-waisted, three-inches-above-the-knee dress and began to laugh again and retreated.

Mum was to be at the course by 10 a.m. to organise an early meal for arrivals who brought horses from places as far away as Seymour. Before that she had to fill the cakes with cream in the cool of the morning and send them away packed in boxes on the tray of the hotel truck that was picking up the foodstuffs from all the womenfolk of the town. Then she must leave everything in readiness for the guard on the 'Beetle' who had offered to 'do' the train for her and the guard on the goods train who had promised likewise. But before she left our hats and dresses were spread on the bed ready for us; mine, pink cotton with white piqué collar and cuffs and my old white hat done up with a new ribbon band. Mick's dress had been let down, let out and titivated till it looked like new to match her new hat.

As soon as Mum and Dad left for the course we got into this finery and went over to the Marvels' place. All morning Mick rode one of the trotters round the paddock and when it was time to leave for the races her dress was wrinkled, concertinaed and dirty.

'What's wrong with it?' she complained when I said it looked awful. Mick's adolescence was passing without the faintest discomfort to her. She was too preoccupied with the fun of living to have time to spare for it. That morning her long legs had hung down eighteen inches past those of her friends the Martin twins, as the three of them rode on the one horse round Marvels' paddock, but she felt no embarrassment. Her new straw hat was nice but she had twirled it round on the end of her forefinger stuck up in the crown and now it had spiralled up to a peak like a witch's hat. She had a small head and couldn't keep the hat on, so put the elastic band under her chin instead of behind her hair.

As for me, the Marvels had helped me achieve – with a new toilette – an elegance of appearance that made me long to know the meaning of the words *dernier cri*, which I'd seen in a book under an illustration that I thought I now resembled. The fullness of the skirt was pulled to the back leaving the front flat and tight. The back was bunched into a sort of bustle and the whole thing cinched in with the belt till I could scarcely breathe. The white panama hat that pulled right down on my head with a brim sticking out for three inches was now unrecognisable. A dent in the crown of the type slashed into men's hats lifted the whole creation up high on my head. The brim was turned up at the back and pulled down in the front over one eye. The pink ribbon was dispensed with entirely. I should have liked to dispense too with the long cotton stockings, but that would have taken more courage than I possessed. Stockings and legs were matters of modesty.

On the way to the races, cars and jinkers passed us on the dirt road. Dust hung like a ribbon along where we walked. We could have moved over closer to the fence and avoided it, but we just didn't want to miss anything. There were horses in boxes behind some of the cars, jockeys rode other horses at a high-legged canter, people we had never seen before went by. A kid in a passing car threw an apple core and it hit Mick and she picked it up with a handful of dust to throw it back, but the hot air of the passing cars tossed the dust back over us. We were hot and perspiration ran in gutters down our dusty cheeks. Mick's perspiration-wet hair hung like rats'-tails, mine looked like a deflated black umbrella.

I knew better than to go near Mum in my 'improved' outfit. I waited at the side of the luncheon booth while Mick went in for orders. I could hear Mum speaking. She said we were not to go near the bookmakers, we were not to speak to strange men, we were not to go to any cars with strange men or women, and to remember that there were men drinking here and *you know what that means*, and do not sit on the seat until you have put paper on it, and here is a shilling each and run along and enjoy yourselves because I'm busy. In the gloom and bustle of the tent she hardly noticed Mick, who came out and repeated the speech to me as, 'Here's a shilling.'

50

This shilling didn't go far, even in those days. We bought a saveloy and a roll (the roll was the great attraction – I hadn't seen one before). Then we bought two navel oranges and a bag of lollies and a bottle of raspberry soda which looked like pink froth when you shook it and made you sick when you drank it. Then we heard a loud wail from the whistle of the goods train away off on the track – cock-a-doodle-doo it went as it rolled down the line, partly in good wishes for the celebration and partly a warning that the ice-cream packed in dry ice had been left at the station. Soon it would be brought here to the races and we had no money. This dilemma was solved in (of all places) the lavatory. The 'Ladies' was a can with a wooden seat in the centre of an arena encircled by a six-foot hessian wall. There was a board outside with LADIES written on it.

We were about to leave the convenience when a lady (we'd never seen her before, as we repeated to each other later) entered. We stepped politely aside for her, but she came to us and gave us threepence to stay outside the entrance and make sure no one came in. We couldn't see the necessity for this.

'I think she wants to change her dress or something,' Mick said, but she didn't stay long and she didn't change her dress.

'Thank you,' she said when she left. 'You are good girls.' Mick charged off with the threepence and bought a Dixie, which we shared. We had just finished this when a second lady approached and said the first lady had told her about us and would we stand guard for her too. Again we collected threepence and again we bought a Dixie. Yet another lady came to us. Oh, we were on to a good thing all right!

But this was the end of our windfall. Through no fault of ours this lady's privacy was not complete: a horse skittered away from the starting line and pranced sideways like a crab with the jockey on its back and turned to bolt only a few feet from us. It propped with the jockey hanging on high in the air above the hessian wall of the lavatory. The woman screamed and raced off pulling her skirt down and completely forgetting that she was in our debt.

Some of the jockeys, we thought, looked like men we knew, but surely they couldn't be, not in those magnificent, flamboyant silks. The start was the best part of the race to watch. They were all there together, the glistening, shining horses, the men glittering, dazzling in their scintillating colours. The bookmakers were yelling incomprehensible jargon and the crowd were yelling to jockeys they knew. Then they were off and that was the last we saw of them for a while as trees and a dip in the ground hid them from view. Interest flagged for a time and many now sauntered off for a drink to wash the dust down.

We saw Dad among the crowd under the bookmakers' umbrellas. He had put two shillings on a horse and he told us its name so we could watch it win.

'These are my daughters,' he told the Melbourne bookmaker.

'Half your luck, mate,' the bookmaker said. Dad told us he would buy us another sav and a roll when his horse won. It didn't, and we knew he didn't have another two shillings so we deserted him.

At what we considered to be afternoon teatime by the state of our stomachs we went across to Mum. She was just coming out of the tent with the other women for a breather. In the blinding sunlight she saw us and stopped, staring.

'Dear God help me,' she sighed aloud as she took in our ensembles.

That night the race ball was held in the Waaia hall. This hall was quite familiar to us kids. The school concerts were held there and we'd played the piano and sung and danced there many a time. While the men got the fire going in the open fireplace in the little supper room out at the back and filled the kerosene tins ready for tea and coffee, the big boys scraped slivers from candles and we slid up and down the floor on a stone-filled box bound with an old blanket to make the boards slippery.

Mum had put the flat irons on the stove when we got home from the races and sponged and pressed Mick's dress back to respectability and brushed her hair till it shone like copper. My belt was let out ('Phew!' Dad expelled air as it was levered off), my curls were re-done, stockings washed and dried in the oven. Mum wore a pink ankle-length voile frock, Dad his navy blue suit. We had had six visitors for tea; two were fettlers but the other four were strangers – Mum had heard them say they were staying for the ball so she had asked them home. Their two big cars stood opulently outside our home. I hoped everyone would see them. We didn't ever own a car.

Because it was a pleasant, clear night we all walked to the hall half a mile away. In the cool air the mingling smell of the berries and flowers of the male and female pepper-corn trees was fresh and cleansing after the dust of the day. Curlews cried and keened on the edges of the wheat paddocks. The lantern hanging from the verandah of the Waaia Hotel flickered brightly through the newly cleaned glass. Mrs Beswick, the proprietor of the hotel, whom we called Mrs B, was to come with us. Mum considered it was somehow respectable here to have a publican for a friend, whereas she considered that it wasn't elsewhere. Out came Mrs B, her big bosom gleaming in the moonlight in a white satin dress. Some Sunday nights she would ask Mum and Dad to play euchre and we kids would watch that bosom. As the game began she would lift it onto the table with both hands and it would move slowly across a large area like molten lead and then, as if it had cooled down, would cease flowing and heave to a standstill. Each time Mrs B dealt the cards this mass would move. Our Mum was a neat little person, a tightly corseted contrast to this undisciplined bulk. Now, apart from the bosom, there was something else about Mrs B. She was smoking!

When I read now of the 'flaming twenties' I feel we must have missed them, because this was the only woman I saw smoke. The few I saw wearing lipstick at this time were definitely regarded as being 'bad' in our circle. But Mrs B was 'different' because she was a friend.

Everyone came to the Waaia Race Ball. Mrs Marvel came dressed in the outfit she milked in, the Morans from out Broken Creek way in their outdated finery they'd brought with them when they arrived from Ireland.

53

When the music struck up for the first dance most of the kids raced round grabbing each other and set off dancing together. The adults avoided them as best they could. Dad took Mum by the arm and began to waltz. Most of the women had partners. Alex Walker, who had ridden a winner today and who could whistle up any bird in the bush so well that he later became famous all over Australia for it, asked Mickie to dance. I thought she would be awful; she looked like a crane with her long, gangly legs. But no, she moved with amazing grace on the floor.

Everything was wonderful, the music, the movement, the dance. And then: 'May I have the pleasure of this dance?' I was being invited to dance! I was eight years old and short and round and didn't get on too well with other kids, but I was being asked to dance!

It was 'old' Bill Leaf, an elderly, small-scale squatter. I wanted to dance. Instead I said, 'I can't dance.' I'd heard about Mr Leaf's dancing. They said he could waltz better than anyone in the district.

'You never thought your sister could move like that till she took the floor, did you?' he said. 'You'll be able to move like that. Come on now.'

Then I was away – 1, 2, 3 – 1, 2, 3 – 1, 2, 3 – balancing on one foot then the other.

'Right now, round we go,' the old man said. 'Long, shortshort, long, shortshort', round and round we went. Once he began circling he didn't stop, round and round and round. He held me in the very old manner, my right arm doubled behind my back, my left hand on his upper arm. I was so secure I didn't falter and when the music stopped I clapped and clapped for it to start again. A sleeper-cutter was playing the gumleaf and a railway fencer had a concertina. They both knew us Smiths and began to play again and off we went once more – 1, 2, 3 – 1, 2, 3 – 1, 2, 3.

'Long, shortshort, long, shortshort, hold your head up, never look at your feet, back straight, heels off the ground. You might

54

have eggshells pinned under your heels when you're in competitions.' Tight little circles round and round.

When it ended he told me I was good. 'You move as well as your sister.' I raced over to Mickie.

'Did you see me?'

'Old Bill Leaf's got grandchildren.'

'Alex Walker's got his teeth out.'

Kevin was sitting on the edge of the stage learning to play the gumleaf. I said to him, 'Did you see me?'

'Yes,' he said. 'Can you hear this?' He was playing 'I'll string along with you', and I could recognise it.

Later a sleeper-cutter took me up in a three-hop polka. 1, 2, 3 hop, 1, 2, 3 hop, round and round, arms gripping arms. Every now and then my partner would give a high call like a highland dancer, and we'd laugh and go at it harder still. Faster and faster grew the music. The concertina-player was sweating and he wiped his brow on his shirt-sleeve without missing a beat. The axeman playing the gumleaf would 'blow' one and reach in his pocket for another and fix it to his lips and blow the reed-like music again.

> See me dance the polka,
> Just see me twirling around,
> See me dance the polka,
> My feet scarce touch the ground,

sang my partner. 'That's the first song Nellie Melba sang in public. She was at a school concert.'

Dancing stopped while supper was handed around, the men carrying big trays with the tea and coffee and the women and children carrying cakes and sandwiches.

'A real blowout', was how Dad described the supper. There were sausage rolls and sandwiches, sponges four inches high filled with cream, sponge rolls, Napoleon cakes, custard slices, chocolate éclairs, meringues, sponge kisses, lamingtons, jelly cakes, and 'wheat stacks' (a name Kevin had given to the big three-deckers of chocolate, vanilla and raspberry-coloured cake joined with whipped cream and iced all over with chocolate icing dusted with coconut, which before serving were cut into manageable slices).

There had been two 'sets' before supper, square dances, four couples to each set. They'd had the Waltz of Cotillons and the Fitzroy Quadrilles. Now Mr Leaf, who was MC, called, 'Ladies and gentlemen. Take your partners for the Lancers!' All the young men shouted, 'Yahoo!' and dived for the liveliest girls. Five sets soon filled, then three couples looked for a fourth. Mr Leaf took my arms and called, 'I'll lead from the floor.' The concertina burst straight into 'Dixie' and we were off.

'Ladies and gentlemen, salute your partner!' We bowed, Mr Leaf to me, me to the old man.

'Oh, I wish I were in the land of cotton, where old friends are not forgotten,' sang the concertina-player.

'Salute the opposite corner, return to your partner and swing!' ordered Mr Leaf.

'Look away, look away, look away, Dixie land.'

'Swing your partner.' This was wonderful. There could be nothing better than this! Round and round we swung, kicking for momentum with one foot while the other pivoted round. Bill Leaf held me as he had when we waltzed with my arm doubled behind my back. All the others swung holding hands, their arms extended to full length. A girl in one of the other sets swung off the floor, her legs hung out behind her as her partner kept swinging her round and round by her hands.

'She's good,' I marvelled to Bill Leaf as we went steadily round and round.

'A good dancer never loses her feet,' he said, and went on round and round, his clenched fist pushed into the small of my back supporting me as I lent on my doubled-back arm. I knew then that we were swinging faster than anyone in the hall and that I could never 'lose my feet' while this old man held me.

Then, 'Ladies to the right, gentlemen to the left. Round you go. Circle twice and lead your partner back to position.'

The music changed. 'There's a track, winding back, to an old-fashioned shack, along the road to, Gundagai.'

'Waaia!' yelled the young men.

'First and third gentlemen promenade your partner.'

'. . . where the blue gums are growing, and the . . . Broken Creek is flowing,' the boys sang on, improvising to fit Waaia's geography into the song.

Dad had a barn-dance with me. He wasn't near so good a dancer as Mum, but what he lacked in skill he made up for with enthusiasm. Holding his partner's arm shoulder-high at right-angles to the body he swept round whacking people left and right with outstretched arms.

'I see you're doing a line with old Bill Leaf,' Dad said. 'You couldn't have got a better bloke to teach you.'

Too soon they called the last dance. It was 2 a.m. and many had long distances to travel home.

'Ladies and gentlemen, take your partners for the last dance, the Medley!'

I asked Kevin for this dance. He'd been to Waaia Race Balls before and could dance well. The gipsy tap, schottische, polka, mazurka, valeta, circular waltz, Pride of Erin, keel row, military two-step, finishing with the three-hop polka. Faster and faster went the polka, but no one left the floor.

The concertina finished 'Little Brown Jug' and the gumleaf player stepped forward. With both hands to the leaf covering his lips he began 'Auld Lang Syne'. Led by Bill Leaf we formed a circle and held hands slowly circling, everyone singing:

> Should auld acquaintance be forgot,
> And never brought to mind?
> Should auld acquaintance be forgot,
> And auld lang syne?
>
> For auld lang syne, my dear.
> For auld lang syne,
> We'll take a cup of kindness yet,
> For auld lang syne.

Mrs B sang solo then as she evidently always did on these

nights. I never knew anyone else besides her who knew the last two verses:

> We two have run about the braes,
> And pulled the gowans fine,
> But we've wandered many a weary foot
> Since auld lang syne.
>
> We two have paddled in the burn,
> From morning sun till dine;
> But seas between us broad have roared
> Since auld lang syne.

Then we crossed hands and moved our arms up and down, moving closer and closer, and pulled the circle tighter together as we sang:

> And there's a hand, my trusty friend
> And gie' us a hand of thine
> And we'll take a cup of kindness yet
> For auld lang syne.

And the Waaia races were over for another year.

10

MESSAGE IN GREEN

The Morans were the only people of 'quality' to live in Waaia. There were other people of substantial means who owned big properties, but they were 'colonials' and even then 'colonial' wasn't considered 'quality'.

We saw little of this family; they held themselves aloof and when tragedy came to them no one knew how to help. Not that help would have been easy even had they not been so far removed from things we were familiar with. In the tragedy that struck them it was hard to know how to help or give sympathy. And ever after this time it was hard to remember that this had been a family we were in awe of because they were 'quality'. I remember years later my pretty cousin Mary racing in to say breathlessly to Mum, 'Auntie Birdie, there's a most beautiful lady up on the station; a real lady.'

Mickie sauntered in hard on her heels and said, to provoke her, 'The old bag of rags.'

Mum said, 'Kathleen!'

'Well,' said Kathleen-cum-Mick, 'she's got a bee in her bonnet, anyway.'

They were both right. It was Joan Moran. She came into the station once a week driving a spring cart. She sat with a ramrod for a backbone on the cross-bar seat of the dray. She wore a ground-length gown of heavy black silk pinched in at the waist and ornamented with jet braiding on the shoulders and down the leg o' mutton sleeves to the wrist. Her black toque sat high on her abundant hair; a gossamer veil bound it lightly down round her chin and covered her face to shield her complexion from the sun and wind. As she stepped down, holding her long skirt genteelly with one hand, you could see her black stockings above the level of her high lace-up boots. She looked absolutely regal.

But, 'She's high,' said my sister.

'Kathleen!' said Mum.

'What about the cream?'

There was no denying that. For all that she still affected the elegant dress of fine people, Joan Moran was filthy. Waiting to be collected on the platform were two cans of cream sent back from the butter factory untouched. Pasted round them was a label with big green lettering: OUR MESSAGE IN GREEN: SEND CLEAN CREAM.

Joan in our time at Waaia tried to sell her produce to Nathalia, Numurkah and Tallangatta butter factories, but always the result was the same: they refused it.

Though the slightest speck of dirt upset Mum she always tried to be generous towards this woman and forbade us to show her any disrespect as other kids did when she passed by.

Joan Moran came from Ireland with her family when she was a young woman. There was Mr Moran, his wife, Joan, and her beautiful sister Teresa. They brought their furniture with them from the Old Country and folk who had seen their home on the banks of the Broken Creek said it was the finest ever brought to our part of Victoria. Old man Moran wore a top hat and a morning coat. Mrs Moran and the two girls dressed in the most expensive and elegant – even though dated – clothes we ever saw on those red dirt roads. There were other things about the family that were full of splendour in our eyes, but the most titillating was that the beautiful Miss Teresa was sent to Melbourne to be educated though she was at least seventeen years old – as old as some of our schoolteachers had been! We learnt that this was called going to 'finishing school'.

In the evening, after tea, when the warm dusk was closing in, I'd play round the only fruit tree we owned, a nectarine to which I ascribed mystical qualities, and pretend that I too was going to finishing school and was learning to walk without running and to wear expensive clothes with ease as did Teresa and Joan Moran. For Joan in the first days of our time at Waaia was a fine young woman only eclipsed in our eyes by the beauty of Teresa.

But all that Teresa Moran learnt at finishing school profited her nothing. Shortly after 'finishing' she married, and three weeks after the ceremony returned home to Broken Creek and didn't leave again. No one outside the family knew what had happened, though everyone made a wild guess.

The Morans took up property in the area that was the original site for Waaia, on Broken Creek, two miles or so from the present town. The word Waaia is Aboriginal for water, and here, where the 'creek' which ran only intermittently in other places was as wide as a river, the first settlers came. The Morans had their property on the far side of the wide creek; no one else lived out there except the Dixon family, who lived on the Waaia side of the water. There was Mr Dixon, Mrs Dixon, and their son.

The Dixons were poor and common; the Morans 'gentry'. They had nothing in common that Waaia knew of. Then one day Mr Dixon murdered Teresa, firing across the wide, deep

61

creek, watched to see her die on the grass, then crawled into a funeral pyre he had built for his own cremation, set it alight and shot himself as the flames burned up around him.

What we made out of those few brief facts was probably no more unlikely than the true story must have been. We believed Mr Dixon – ugly and ordinary as he was – was Teresa's lover, but because each was already married they were destined never to be together. We believed – especially those of us with enough Irish to know what a fickle paddy such a situation could arouse – that Teresa taunted him until he could bear it no longer.

Mrs Dixon was working as a charwoman for Mrs Young, the wheat-buyer's wife. It was near sundown and she was walking the two miles back to her home when she saw the great blaze in the tepee-like pile of wood her husband had been building. She ran back to Mrs Young.

'I know what's in that fire,' she gasped. 'My man's there, dead. I heard a gun. Now I know why he built that hollow stack of wood, now I know.'

By the time the police had been summoned from Numurkah, there was a murder as well as a suicide to investigate, because by now Teresa's body had been found.

On the afternoon of her death the beautiful Teresa had been asked to bring in the cows. When she didn't return by nightfall Joan was sent to see what was keeping her. Joan told us later what she found, told us in the almost incoherent, jumbled speech left her by the shock.

'Our Teresa should not die,' she struggled to say. 'Lying there, blood-soaked grass, blood-soaked Teresa, gossners [geese] blood-soaked, everywhere near the water by herself.'

The police sifted the ashes of the fire and after the inquest Mrs Dixon and her son were allowed to take the box of remains in their jinker and bury them in the cemetery in Numurkah.

'He always said she was an Irish bitch,' Mrs Dixon said in our kitchen once. Mum tut-tutted; no one used that sort of language in her hearing. 'He hated her. He thought she put her cows in our paddock after dark. He used to go out night after night to make sure she didn't do that. "She's an Irish bitch," he used to tell me. I think she made googly eyes at him. He wouldn't have anything to do with her.'

That great blazing pyre on one side of the water and the body of the beautiful Teresa on the other were the subject of much talk, but no more could be added than was already general knowledge.

We had never known the Morans. Their aristocratic bearing created a social moat around them that even tragedy could not ford. Mrs Dixon and her son moved into a little three-roomed cottage in the town, but the Morans stayed on in their big home by the creek. They were not part of us; they were foreign, not because of their nationality, not altogether because of their affluence, but more because of their certainty of life always providing for them. They were not part of that uncertainty that the Depression forced on the rest of us, binding us surely if loosely. Some of the Waaia people had no work; the father of the Green family who lived near the railway gates was away humping his bluey looking for a job; others had only seasonal work lumping wheat. Because Dad had a permanent job we were almost in the aristocrat class ourselves, more comfortable than the wheat-farmers certainly, for they never knew for how long they'd be able to hang on: one error in selling too soon or holding too long was all those times allowed.

It wasn't until after the old gentleman and lady Moran died that the barrier was broken. Joan didn't frighten us at all now, because we had something in common; she was a battler like the rest of us. Under the terms of her parents' will and because the death of Teresa had unseated her mind, Joan was not allowed the handling of the estate or of any money. The church in Numurkah was made trustee until her death. All accounts had to be forwarded there. Joan was so lonely and lost that she sought the companionship of others even though, because of her upbringing more than her recent affliction, she was unable to reciprocate. She would drive in with her can of cream and pull

63

up and talk to anyone she saw, sad and lonely and a bit careless now in her dress, but still at this stage clean in her person.

Then a suitor arrived. The news flashed round the town like a lightning strike. He was young, not too bad-looking, and he was helping her with the farm. And then he had gone and it was all over.

Some boys duck-shooting on the creek said they had seen police and a lawyer out there talking to him. The rumour ran that he was after Joan's money, that he had coaxed her to marry him. Whatever his intention his attention had brightened Joan up considerably. She was dressing as she had in the old days and was speaking almost normally again.

On her own once more, there was nothing to save Joan. At first when we saw her dirt we thought it was accidental, but soon it was obvious that her mind was as unseated as it had been before the coming of the suitor; worse, she was reverting to the animal. Great drooling dogs hung round her, geese sat on her lap – two of them were curled up with her one day when she arrived in the spring cart. They looked a little dismayed at the length of the journey as they squatted beside the dirty woman.

'They be Teresa's gossners,' she told us.

In the heat of mid-summer she drove in, dressed in her elegant clothes, pinched in tightly at the waist, high-necked, with long tight sleeves and a tiny toque fastened on with the gossamer veil. The veil was sticking to her face with dust and perspiration.

'Could I have a mug of water, missus,' this graceful apparition asked as she climbed down.

'No, Joan,' Mum said tenderly. 'Today you'll come to my house and have a cup of tea.'

Mum sat her in the kitchen and we sat there too, staring when Mum wasn't watching. And then as Mum handed her a cup of tea I saw a movement on her shoulder and two beetle-like insects walked down her sleeve. Mum turned away. I thought she was going to be sick. She couldn't eat anything, just drank her tea and tried not to look at Joan.

After Joan left, Mum ordered Mickie and me to take the chair she had been sitting on outside and then all the other chairs, and these we must scrub.

'Did you see them?' she gasped. 'The bugs on her arm. Don't stand there' – this last to me who was interested in anything that crawled – 'go and wash yourself . . . take your clothes off and air them.' Mum wasn't herself for days after.

Next week when Joan came to the station she brought a gift of a half-pound of tea, a tin of sugar and a pat of home-made butter, a sort of saffron shade that smelt like her cream. This set Mum off again; she changed colour before our eyes. As soon as Joan drove off Mum hurried down from the station holding the pat of butter at arm's length and dropped it down the lavatory.

Her panic wasn't without cause. Strange tales were being told of Joan. The police from Numurkah had visited her one day following a complaint and found she was slaughtering and storing the carcasses of calves in her house to feed her dogs. The house, they found, was filthy beyond cleansing. The trustees were contacted and she was ordered to move out of the old homestead to a little cottage they built her. Joan moved some of the furniture over but still slept in the old place.

One Sunday Kevin and I went out to Broken Creek. We were going to sneak up to Joan's house and peep through the windows. We got as far as her rickety old gate tied with wire and all her dogs began to bark and her geese to scream. You never heard such a commotion. Geese flew from old farm machinery, out of the trees, up from the creek and out the door of the house. Hideous great dogs lolloped out baying, a battalion of starved mongrels with their ribs almost sticking through their diseased and scabby skins, froth erupting from their mouths. Kevin and I ran so fast we were out of sight of the house before we stopped for breath. We never went back again and we never told anyone of our visit.

A few weeks after this there was a mission at the church in

Numurkah. We never missed a mission. They were the highlights of our liturgical year. Though we had to drive in in the dark with old Billy harnessed to the jinker, it was worth it. We sang all the way in and slept all the way home. This night the church was ablaze with lights and the coloured glass windows were warm and festive. People milled about and everyone knew we were the Smiths from Waaia and had driven ten miles in and would drive ten miles home that night, and they waved to us and asked us to supper afterwards and shook Dad's hand. Dad always came to the mission, as many non-Catholics did. We always had someone extra to squeeze into the jinker. This night it was a friend of Mickie's, Rene Martin.

Rene was sitting gaping round at the decorations, the altar sparkling with the hundred candles, flowers in tall silver vases, low bowls with sprays trailing down to the red carpeted floor, statues of angels and saints and the Virgin and Jesus and Joseph, all gaily painted. And in the centre of this constellation of light the great gold monstrance that held the exposed sacrament for the duration of the mission scintillated with a brilliance that dimmed all else. Rene had her head stuck out the end of the seat to see all this and suddenly she gave a cry as a figure went by down the aisle.

'There's old Joan!' she cried aloud.

And sure enough there was Joan Moran in her floor-length dress, her gossamer veil anchoring her elegant hat of thirty years ago on her red bird's-nest hair.

Old Mrs Dixon lived on in the town for a few months only. Then, one day, just before the train was due, Mum called me. 'Go quickly. Tell Mrs Young that Mrs Dixon is dead. I'll meet her there.'

Mrs Young ran up the road, still with her apron on, to the little cottage, and I ran after her. By the time I got to the door I could hear her praying. She was down on the floor where the dead woman still lay, shouting into her ear. It was the Confiteor she was saying, hoping that its words of supplication would penetrate any spirit still alive in the now dead body. I walked back to the road. Still I could hear her: 'I confess to Almighty God . . . that I have sinned exceedingly in thought, word and deed. Through my fault, through my fault, through my most grievous fault.'

Out on the road I struck my breast three times from habit.

11

THE TRANSPLANTED SHAMROCK

O nce a year I held the floor at school, no matter where we lived. I would stand up before the end of the day and announce that I would not be coming to school for two weeks.

'We are going on holidays.'

I never knew anyone else who had holidays; certainly no one went away as we did. We could travel interstate to one destination and return on our pass, but in our home State we could have stayed on trains for the whole two weeks travelling from one end of the country to the other. We virtually did this.

Mum's seven sisters and one surviving brother all lived on farms at one time or another, and many of them worked, or had worked, on the railways. They were scattered from Nullawil in the north-west of the State to Cabbage Tree Creek in the south-east. They were a close-knit family and circulated freely between one another. We circulated annually. Dad's family was not so clannish and had fragmented to such a degree that they were spread from Perth in Western Australia to Beaudesert in Queensland and down to King Island in Bass Strait. Those who were not farming were in timber-milling, having all been brought up in the big timber country round Noojee in Gippsland. Thus we had a number of calls to make, a plurality of towns to visit and exciting occupations to investigate.

But the first journey of the two weeks was always to the two grandmothers who lived in Gippsland: Grandmother Adams in Longwarry, Granny Smith in Warragul.

For me, the travelling was certainly better than the arriving. We'd start off on the 'Beetle' at 4 p.m., change to the steam train at Numurkah, and arrive at Spencer Street late at night. Then we'd troop across the street to the Batman Hill Hotel where the owner's wife, after taking one look at us, would put us into an upstairs room where there was a double and two single beds.

'The little girls won't want to be alone in a strange city,' she kindly reasoned.

While we waited the following day for the train that would take us to Gippsland, we'd have a pie and a cup of tea at the Flinders Street station cafeteria. Mick and I always took a tooth-pick from the jar on the cashier's desk and ostentatiously picked our teeth as we walked the platform. No one could say we didn't know what to do in the Big Smoke!

Grandmother Adams was small and dainty and pretty and narrow-minded, and I didn't like her much. She felt the same about me, and because she was old and could think quicker she usually got the last word in, first. I was building make-believe houses with the needles from her pine trees once and showed a young cousin how to do the same. When Grandmother called us for tea she saw the results and said to my cousin, 'That's a nice house.' To me she said, 'Are you trying to copy her?'

69

We had only one thing in common: we admired the pioneering spirit. She would tell me stories by the hour of the pioneering days, and I would listen for as long as she would talk. She and my grandfather had pioneered the hills of Gippsland.

It is a sad commentary on our national outlook that the poor are never mentioned in the annals of pioneering history. These people were given no grants, assigned no servants. They took up and paid for land that the wealthy (and often absent) landowners had rejected because it was worthless or too isolated to expect people to live and work on it. They built slab huts with an 'earth' floor. They took work where they could find it to buy their first couple of cows, and the women and children milked the cows while the father went shearing, fencing – anything to try to make ends meet, for cow-cockying never did. And when they lost that place, as lose they mostly did, they moved further back to land even more isolated and barren and therefore cheaper and began again.

Surely that spirit is worth recording.

Grandmother Adams had been burnt out twice in the Gippsland hills. Once she narrowly escaped with her life. My grandfather was away.

'I sent your aunt Anastasia to ride to neighbours to tell them we needed help; the fire was surrounding us. Not long after she left, the wind changed. I looked at the track she had taken and now flames criss-crossed it and as I watched a blazing tree fell right across it. She was a wonderful horsewoman, you know, and I knew she'd get to the neighbours but I thought she'd never get back. The bigger children helped me pull my sewing machine outside and we covered it with wet bags and I gathered up what we could carry. As we left the house I looked across to the only gap that was clear of flames and there was your aunt, sailing high over a fallen log, her horse bringing her home at the gallop.

'"How did you find that opening?" I asked her.

'"I followed the two men," she said.

'"What men? There's no men here."

'"Oh yes, they jumped the log ahead of me. When the wind

changed I didn't know which way to go and these men rode out ahead and beckoned me to follow them." '

My grandmother always blessed herself at this stage.

'There had been no men. It was God Himself that led that girl home.'

But men did come through the gap after her and they brought horses.

'We strapped a mattress on each of the two horses' backs and I ran with the baby covered in a wet shawl. Sparks caught a mattress and it went up in flames.

'While the men were dragging it off the horse's back we heard the other horse scream. The mattress on its back had caught afire too and before the men could stop it it galloped straight into the blazing forest with the burning saddle strapped to its back.'

Whenever I thought of that scene it was my aunt Stasia that I could see. For as long as I remember her she was an austere, dignified woman. I never heard her measured, organ-like voice or watched her stately ramrod-backed walk but I thought of that ride and that brave leap over the smouldering log when she was a young and beautiful girl, 'the belle of the Gippsland Hills'.

It was Grandmother Adams who told me of the struggles of the Irish.

'Never forget what the English did to the Irish,' she said. Yet hanging on her kitchen wall was a picture of Queen Alexandra and another of Queen Mary.

'Yes, well,' she'd say, 'they're different.'

One day when she was saying she'd never lift a finger to help England I reminded her that her sons Stephen and Jack had died fighting for England at Gallipoli. But that was 'different' too.

She had a lot of superstition and folk-lore that probably came from her mother, my great-grandmother, who, she told me, smoked a little clay pipe secretly, hiding it in her cupped hand.

One day when I was older I was cutting up raw steak for a sea-pie. I was feeling miserable and told her I was menstruating. She ordered me to put the meat down at once.

'Never handle meat when you're having your monthlies,' she warned me. 'It will turn it bad.'

Her favourite reply when we'd ask what was for the next meal was, 'Bread and point.' This originated, she told me, from a common Irish meal, potatoes being a substitute for bread. 'When the British were starving the Irish out all we had was our crop, our potatoes. Mothers would cook potatoes and put them on the plates. In the centre of the table she'd put a small piece of cheese or bacon; some hung an onion from a string down from a hook in the ceiling. You'd stick your fork into a potato and point it at the tasty thing and that would make your mouth water and you'd taste the thing you were pointing at and it would aid the digestion of the potatoes.'

She told me of living at Bungaree when she was a child. Bungaree is near Ballarat and is now a rich agricultural area.

'Bungaree was a little Ireland. We'd all come out when the blight struck and the crops failed. The boys there were a lively lot. They took their politics seriously. It was a brave politician trod the boards at Bungaree! A man came there once, Billy Hughes I think it was, all for having conscription brought in on our poor boys [quite forgetting her own three sons had volunteered for that same war]. Anyway, they tipped up his platform and threw chairs and there were fights everywhere and his cronies whisked him away just in time. Well, a few weeks later this same man was speaking in Ballarat. "Citizens of Ballarat," he began. "Savages of Bungaree." The name stuck; Bungaree Savages we were and proud of it.'

Granddad Adams was a big man, and very strong. Sometimes he'd pick me up by the back of my dress at the waist and carry me around that way with one big hand while he fed the horses. He had beautiful horses. Punch and Prince were two that would have carried off prizes at any show. Sometimes he'd run short of tank water for them and he'd yoke one of the horses to the little iron furphy and we'd go to the butter factory for water.

'Look at the way Prince lifts his feet,' he'd say. 'Look at the neck!' On the little iron tank of the furphy was a plaque with

The new family: Dad, Mum, Miss Mickie and me. Mum made the hats from cabbage-tree fronds.

Opposite (top): *'Big Lizzie' rolled across the desert of the Sunset Country, flattening the scrub that struggled to hold the sand together.*

Opposite (bottom): *The promised land of the Mallee – 'fit for heroes' – was turned into a dust bowl by extensive clearing. In nine years the men hadn't got a crop and couldn't pay for the hire and transport of horses and equipment so were driven off.*

'We mightn't have much money but we can make a lot of fun' was Dad's motto. Picnics and rabbit hunts in the desert were our big days out. Mum was as good a shot as any.

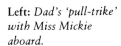

Left: *Dad's 'pull-trike' with Miss Mickie aboard.*

Below: *Railway yards became our playground. Cousin Nancy Buick (left), Miss Mickie and I are off for a ride at Nullawil.*

Above: *Aged four, on Billy, at Briagalong. We rode from the time we walked.*

Left: *On Waaia at Waaia.*

Left: *Back to Waaia and Kevin's tricycle is swamped with me, tin dish and dipper. Everyone said I was 'sprouting up'.*

Below: *Mum (left) was station-mistress wherever we went, and Miss Mickie (right) was sometimes her 'reliever'. Friend Lil Jorgenson (centre) also 'relieved' when we went on the annual holiday provided by Victorian Railways.*

Left: *By Miss Mickie's clothes and Dad in trousers instead of working dungarees it must be Sunday. The tank-stand made of railway sleepers doubled as a wash-stand and cream separator; here some of our pet cockatoos wait to drink from the milk bucket. The only water tap in our world was on this small tank.*

Below: *The Last Dance, Penshurst, 1939. Mrs Twomey and Mrs Hopkins 'presented' us.*

Débutantes & Partners at the Parish Ball Penshurst   June 27th 193

The war swept us all away. That life we had
known was gone forever.

the motto engraved, 'Good, better, best, never let it rest, until your good is better and your better best.'

Grandmother Adams had long ago tired of Granddad and he was never at his best in the house. He had a big walrus moustache and a moustache cup which had a sort of verandah to keep the whiskers out of the tea, but invariably he would get them wet and have to wring them out with his fingers. The ends of the white whiskers were orange from pipe smoking. The pipes hung in a rack beside the kitchen stove and smelt badly. Grandmother had never got used to them in a home where everything was spotless and polished. These smelly, grubby, chewed pipes called forth many caustic comments.

'Has someone trodden in something nasty or is it the pipes?' she would say if she were displeased with him.

As for his spittoon – that was the cross of her life.

'Holy Father in Heaven,' she'd say when she heard the loud 'Splop!' as Granddad aimed across to the big saucer-like receptacle. 'Dear God!' Sometimes: 'Holy Mother of God!'

Granddad had none of the bushman's philosophy and the only time I heard anything approaching such wisdom from him was when I innocently asked him about his ancestry. 'I heard the women talking last night,' I said. 'They said we were all descended from a President of the United States.' I wasn't very impressed by this. America was not a nation of such account in those days. I was interested only because I'd read at school that the second President of the USA was named John Adams, as was my grandfather, and many of the names of that American Adams family were the names of the men of Granddad's family.

He turned on me quite angrily: 'If the only good part of you is your ancestors you're no better than a potato, the best part of you under the ground.' He never mentioned it again and neither did I, but I marked his wise words, the only quote I ever heard from him.

Most of his stories were of early days in the bush. He told me of the strikes and lock-outs of the 1890s.

'The squatters tried to starve us out but we never gave in till our hides were cracking. I walked home from the Queensland border once. I'd sold my saddle-horse and my pack-horse for food and boot leather. It was a long tramp. And when I got home there was no cheque to hand over. Christmas had come and gone and Bridget had managed somehow. I think there must have been a bit of that bread and point she tells you about.'

These stories of my grandparents made me admire them, even wish to emulate their bravery and to tell people of their exploits in helping pioneer this once wild country, but that was the only thing I was happy about when I stayed with them. I felt always the most dreaded uneasiness there as though some day something would happen; what it would be I didn't know, couldn't even imagine, but there was something wrong, and I could tell it as only a child can sense these things. My grandmother was often openly hostile to me. My grandfather never humiliated me but I often caught him looking secretly at me as though he were pondering about me. This unnamed thing made me nervous and apt to be either tongue-tied or garrulous.

THE COLONIAL THISTLE

I t was with relief that I would accompany the family to
Warragul, the home town of Granny Smith. I liked staying
there, as most children would have done; most parents, like
Mum, would be against it.

Granny Smith was the antithesis of Grandmother Adams.
What the neighbours thought never worried her. She wouldn't
have understood the term, 'keeping up with the Joneses'. Life
was no problem to her. She did as she pleased twenty-four hours
a day. She ate when she pleased, went to sleep in front of visitors,
and broke the stuffiest rules of gentility. Her eccentricities were
equalled only by her dignity, a nobility of bearing that set her
apart from the harassed, worry-bent women of her age. She was
very beautiful, tall with fine bones, tapering sensitive fingers and

a tiny waist. In her young days, as photographs we have of her show, she dressed elegantly, her smart ensembles topped always with a toque the like of which Queen Mary later affected. Now, when she was already old (she was forty-six when my father was born), she dressed for comfort; in summer she wore a type of muu-muu, in winter she put on everything she owned.

Born Isabella Hutton in the lowlands of Scotland in 1850 to a wealthy landowning family, she came to Australia with her parents and brothers when she was a young girl in her teens. Squeezed in beside her on her old spring rocking chair I'd listen to stories of her childhood in Scotland, 'an uncoo wild country', she described it, and to tales of Australia in the later gold-rush days. In this chair she told me about Granddad Smith, 'Jem' as she called him. He had died when I was still an infant.

Unaware that the passage of time had annulled the penalty due to him she told me in conspiratorial tones that he had jumped ship in Sydney to look for gold.

'There were notices in all the papers,' she whispered. 'He read some of them to me. "James Adam Smith, Bosun" they had written in big letters. They offered a reward too. You see, they had found gold here and the men all left the ships and went to the diggings and there was no one to take the ships out. When Jem brought me to Melbourne there were scores of ships tied up in the port with not an officer or seaman to man any one of them.'

'How did you come to be in Melbourne, Granny?'

'Jem brought me.'

'Where from?'

'The goldfields.'

Her parents, she told me, while awaiting the ship that was bringing their flocks and shepherds from Scotland, toured about the new country while waiting to take up land.

'My brothers were amusing themselves trying their hand at gold-digging; they each took out a claim, but in a short while we were going on to the place we had made arrangements for before we left Scotland. We were going to raise the same sheep

76

there we had raised on the Cheviot Hills for years without number.'

'But what was Granddad doing in the diggings? Where was he going?'

'He was passing through' – here she'd giggle like a young girl again. 'Putting a distance between Sydney and him.'

I understood his desire for that, but I couldn't understand a runaway seaman and the daughter of landed gentry –

'Your parents let you go with Granddad?'

'No.'

After a while: 'Did you ever see your parents again?'

'No.'

'Didn't you write?'

'I couldn't write. It was Jem who was the educated man.'

'Did you never want to see them again?'

'No, I don't think so.' It was so long ago she couldn't remember. 'I don't think I missed them. So much happened. We went deep in the bush here in Gippsland out Tanjil Bren way. Your grandfather could do anything. He was big and strong.' She had old, faded pictures of him splitting palings in the blackwood forests that stood in Gippsland last century, tree-ferns twenty feet high crowded where he and his mate posed with their broad axes, paling knives, cross-cut saws, mauls and wedges, their crib bags hung on a nearby sapling. (Strange times the birth of our nation saw: grandfather, a runaway ship's bosun; his mate, a lawyer who later took up a lucrative practice in Melbourne.)

There were fourteen children born to the family, and Granny was her own midwife every time, with a neighbour to help her. She was known over a wide area as an excellent midwife and was often called on by doctors for help.

All her sons were good bushmen, handy with the axe and their fists, willing to have a go at anything. My father won a five-mile cross-country race against the top professional runners of the State when he was only fifteen. He ran in an old pair of sandshoes and his school pants.

'Your uncle Teddy could run too but you never knew what he'd do next. A naughty boy was my Teddy!' Granny would chuckle. 'Once, just before the start of a race Jem went to him and told him he'd put ten shillings on him to win. Halfway through the race Teddy was well in the lead. Then he remembered he had himself backed another runner to win so he threw himself flat on the ground and called, "Water, water." Someone took water to him and helped him to his feet just as Jem reached him. "I'll give you water," your grandfather said and swung his fist. He had a good punch, my Jem had. Teddy had to be carried off the ground.'

Uncle Ted was the only member of either side of my huge family tree who lived apart from the marital partner. This would have put him beyond the pale even if it hadn't been that he was a wild, eccentric man who cared no more than Granny for convention or worldly acclaim. He lived at home with Granny now, a huge man with an angry ridge scarred right across his forehead where his skull had once been lifted up and later replaced with crude surgery. Working in the bush in the tall timbers he had fallen from the staging forty feet up and the axe had laid his head clean open. He was brought into the hotel in Warragul and Granny and a doctor closed the gash and clamped it together as best they could. The then young man was conscious.

'There were a lot of men helping me to hold him while the doctor went about his work,' Granny told me.

Uncle Ted's room was always a shambles and I tidied it with a feeling of doing good. He saved his cigarette butts in tins, a habit of the Depression. When I complained he told me of men in the bush who used to flip their butts up to the ceiling where they'd stick by the end moistened from the lips, and there they'd stay until they were swept down in the day of need. He also showed me how men smoked very short butts without burning their fingers by sticking a darning needle in them.

Teddy undoubtedly was the black sheep of the family. I knew by the polite manner with which my mother greeted him. But

I liked him. He gave me the best presents anyone outside my immediate family ever did. Each time I cleaned his room he gave me a gift. Once it was a tiny pair of scissors that folded up to a little packet one inch square. They were not new and Mum was very sceptical as to their origin, but I didn't care of course. Another time he gave me a very much used copy of *Billabong's Daughter*, by Mary Grant Bruce.

'I've had that for nearly eight months waiting for your visit,' he told me. 'I thought it looked the sort of book you'd like.' Mum swiftly recalled that he had recently been employed as a gardener by a family whom she knew had a great collection of books.

'They've probably got one less now,' Dad joked, but Mum never saw the humour in situations involving this 'unfortunate', as she termed him.

No doubt there was much about Granny Smith's life that would upset an adult, but for a child she was wonderful. She enjoyed her food at a period when it was genteel to glue your elbows to your ribs when brandishing a knife and fork and stick your little finger out like a cup-hook when drinking. All this was not for Granny. She could slurp louder than anyone I ever heard. When she drank soup she could actually hold the spoon away from her mouth and with tremendous suction draw it across the gap. She ate and drank everything boiling, so probably this was a cooling method. She had no stove but cooked on an open fire. There was an iron bar across the chimney and long hooks hung down from this to hold the big iron kettle and her iron camp oven. The kettle was always boiling and the oven (a circular iron pot with a close-fitting lid and three little legs) was always simmering. She'd put anything at all in that camp oven. I've seen turnips, beans, potatoes, onions, ox-tail, lambs' brains, oatmeal and left-overs from the day before all put together and left to simmer for the day.

Before I could walk she had given me a big china mug that Dad had given her as a lad when he'd received his first pay. It had green leaves and red holly berries as decoration and the words

REMEMBER ME in gold letters. Each year when I came down on holidays I'd get the mug from her cupboard and show her the dust on it, and we'd both be pleased at this evidence of its not being used since my last visit. I have that mug still.

Though her burr was so thick you could cut it with a knife she hated the bagpipes. Some pipers paraded through our house to celebrate Hogmanay when she was living with us near the end of her life. Fortunately they'd gone before she found her walking-stick.

HO! HO! TALLYGARO!

There was always plenty to amuse us on the long train journeys. Some games were elaborate, but the favourite was simply to cross our fingers when we saw a white horse and keep them crossed until we saw a white dog. Once Mickie travelled from Shepparton to Spencer Street with her fingers crossed, and Mum only persuaded her to uncross them by saying she could begin again at daylight next day.

Another favourite was imitating the noises of the train. Dad always thought up the funniest of these, although Mum's were the more apt. A guard came into our compartment one day and was startled to hear Dad chanting, 'I ought to take his teeth out, I ought to take his teeth out . . .' Mum's train noises often took the form of rhymes using the names of stations we passed through:

Tallygaroopna, Tallygaroopna,
Ho! Ho! Tallygaro!
Tallygaroopna, Tallygaroopna,
Play the game for Tallygaro!

The one of hers we thought brilliant was:

Katamatite, Katamatite
The drunk fell on the bed,
He spoke to his wife whose name was Kate,
'Kate-am-I-tight?' he said.

Sometimes in peak periods we had to travel in the old-style 'dog-boxes', separate little compartments as opposed to carriages with a corridor. The door at each side of the dog-box gave access from platforms at stations. These old carriages had spittoons in the floor, brass funnels let down through the boards, twelve inches in diameter funnelling down to a two-inch outlet. I never saw them used as spittoons (evidently the day of spitters was gone) so I never learnt if others were as adept as my grandfather in their use. People shoved lolly papers down them then; Dad didn't think much of this practice. 'Think of the men having to pick up those papers,' he'd say with a grimace. The dog-boxes didn't have lavatories and it was often a long way between stations and even then problematical whether or not you could get to the lav and back before the train left the station. Hal Gye, who did the wonderful illustrations for *The Sentimental Bloke*, told me that on his first trip to Melbourne from the bush he travelled in such a dog-box, and as the train rattled on through the night he heard a peculiar noise and peering through the gloom (the lights had been extinguished just as we used to do if we wanted to sleep during long night trips) he saw two 'painted women' squatting over the brass spittoons relieving themselves.

Dog-boxes were the exception rather than the rule. Guards seeing our pass which branded us as railway people, and seeing our general appearance which no doubt branded us as bushwhackers if only by our carefreeness and lack of restraint, would try to get us the best seats possible, with windows for us two girls. When we moved from Briagalong to Waaia the train was crowded out of Spencer Street and Mum and Dad were each nursing Mick and me when the guard came along to check tickets. He saw our pass.

'You're going to be tired nursing those kids all night,' he said. 'What time did you knock off?' Dad told him, 5 p.m.

'Starting in the morning at the new place?'

'As soon as I get enough unpacked for the wife to set up house.'

The guard jerked his thumb for us to follow him out into the corridor and led us to the first-class section, which was never crowded. There we sat for the rest of the journey, stiff, uneasy, unspeaking, our poor cases conspicuous among the other valises on the racks above our heads.

Another time, when we were on our way to Bunyip, the guard after checking our pass came back a little later to tell Dad there was another railway family on the train. We all trooped along the corridor to look for them. They weren't hard to find, the man with the badge of the navvy – lumps of flesh off his hands where a 'dog had got him' (the iron dogs used in laying rails), shoulders hunched from carrying weights, his face brown and leathery from the weather.

They were glad to see us. Dad told them of the different places we'd lived on the line, and Oh, yes, they knew of us.

'I worked with Negri from Wingeel on a section a while back,' the man told us. 'Is this the baby he said you brought to Nowingi?'

'Yes,' Mum said proudly.

'Well,' said the other navvy, 'it looks as though you can rear kids as well as Kelly can rear dingo pups!' We all laughed, delighted that the story of the struggle to keep the baby alive in 'woop-woop' had been passed on.

Then there was talk of others we knew.

'If you're going to Bunyip you'll find a cobber of mine in the gang. Used to be with me at Wycheproof. Black by name. Give him my regards and tell him we're still growing pumpkins from the seeds of his big ironbark.' There was a camaraderie between navvies; whether it was the period we were passing through or the age of our young society, or the type of hard, often crippling work, it made no difference to the end result. We had the feeling of 'belonging to a big family', as Harold (later Sir Harold) Clapp, Commissioner for Railways, once said to Dad. To say you were a navvy or the family of a navvy on the line was a passport into companionship.

The two big city stations in Melbourne gave us as much pleasure as anything else in our travels. Flinders Street was good, but Spencer Street was better. Flinders Street was more of a city-dwellers' station; Spencer Street was where most of the lines to the country places that we knew ran from. Mick and I always made ourselves known to the Man in Grey who announced trains as they came and went and answered queries.

'Do you know where So-and-So is?' we'd ask to try his knowledge of whichever outlandish place we were then living in. He knew Nowingi but he didn't know Wingeel. Then, full of assurance we tried – Waaia!

'Waaia?' he said. 'You're making that one up, you little bush rats.' We were delighted. Superciliously we pointed to where it was on the big illuminated map beside his shelter, only of course it wasn't actually marked there. He asked the station-master and the assistant station-masters and none of them knew if what we said was correct until the big 'route' book was produced and there in tiny print was 'Waaia'. When the next inquirer came to him the august Man in Grey introduced us to him as, 'Two young ladies from *Waaia*! What do you think of that?'

All these amusements of travel would cease as we neared home. Coming back to Waaia we would leave the lush green rolling hills of Gippsland and travel into the flat, dry, golden, warm land of the Goulburn Valley, and we sensed, with the sorrow of leaving another holiday behind us, the joy of coming home. Though we had only been gone two weeks we would notice changes.

'The grass is drier,' Mum would lament. 'There'll be nothing left of my flower garden.'

As we rumbled over Dad's section of the line close to home you could see him 'listening' with all his body to the track beneath the train's wheels.

'We'll have to put a bit of ballast here,' and, 'Sounds like a sleeper gone there.'

And then we were back where time moved slowly, and no doubt for city visitors a little dully, but for us, home.

VELLY NICE
FLUIT

The tradesmen who visited us at Waaia were little travelling oases of variety.

There was a Chinese greengrocer who drove his horse-drawn wagon down from Nathalia once a week. He was a small yellow man wearing in winter a black skull-cap and in summer a battered grey felt. He spoke as we expected Chinese to speak – as many English-speaking people still expect them to do.

'Velly nice lipe melon. You tly?' He'd slice off a piece and we'd 'tly'.

'You likey lettucey? You likey clisp ladish? Fluit?'

One day a steam train came shrieking in and took his horse by surprise, which made it rear a little.

'Horse!' said Charlie. 'You likey box on ear?'

He always gave us kids something to eat. Each Christmas he brought a Chinese jar of sweet ginger in syrup as a gift for Mum.

'Happy Clissmus, missus,' he said. 'Happy Clissmus.'

One day Mum said, 'You work hard, Charlie. Why don't you have a rest?'

'Me no lest,' he said earnestly. 'Me savee money. Go home. Die in China.' And he did.

There was a butcher every Friday. He let down the back of his van to form a table with a small chopping block. There were scales hanging from the roof of the van beside the joints. On the floor were dishes of smallgoods.

A fish man who fished in the Murray River came down on occasions to sell his catch. He drove an A Model Ford and had the fish spread out in the back of it on gum boughs with more gum boughs over them to keep the flies and heat away. He brought the succulent red-fin and the great cod that sometimes grew to prodigious size in deep holes in the mighty river.

The Afghan or Indian hawkers with their beautiful turban pins sparkling above their foreheads were later ousted by the practice of catalogue buying, but looking in an illustrated brochure never held the thrill of the cry: 'Quick! An Afghan's coming!'

The sides of the Afghan hawker's wagon divided lengthways, half being fastened up, half down as a counter when he stopped. All his goods were thus displayed. Aprons, house-frocks, socks, children's fleecy-lined pants, men's 'blueys' and dungaree trousers, hats, slippers and towels. It must have taken Eastern sleight of hand to fit the many things into a wagon that one horse must pull.

Sometimes an Afghan would camp in our house paddock and we'd watch his silhouette passing across his camp-fire near the black bulk of his caravan, and all the antique *exotique* of the East encircled us and made us aware of the crude, stimulating newness of our land.

Waaia was on the line to Picola, which is the same as saying it was on the line to nowhere. Yet we had enough travellers to amuse us, and when there was no one else we amused ourselves.

No one much ever came by train except Miss Genevieve Pendleton, Kevin Young's aunt. She came to stay with Mrs Young, her sister. Miss Gen. stepped fresh from the train in what we called 'flash' clothes, meaning they were very smart, and she carried neat, new suitcases. She was companion and confidante to a wealthy Melbourne socialite. This was so far beyond the horizon of our experience that she was always a thing of great wonder to us.

One morning when she was having her early morning cup of tea in bed (in itself a thing of wonder to us because she wasn't sick!) she heard herself being serenaded. For a spinster this was a thing of delight: someone was trilling and warbling a beautifully whistled rendition of 'Genevieve' – 'Oh Genevieve, I'd give the world . . .' She sprang from her bed and ran to the window. There, hobbling by with his hop-and-carry-one was Yorky; only an old, wizened boots at a pub, but able to whistle down the angels – to say nothing of the chagrined Miss Gen.

Old Gran. Pendleton, Kevin's grandfather who lived with the Youngs, was a good storyteller. He'd been in the constabulary in India and would hold us enthralled for hours while he told us of the mutiny and of cavalry charges in his parade-ground voice. He had a Kitchener-type moustache which would quiver as he roared, 'Forward the Foot!'

Sometimes a railway 'home on wheels' was shunted off on to our siding and in this would live a fencer and his mate or two painters. These men who lived a lonely life usually played an instrument or had some other method of entertaining that made them welcome at bush homes. My Uncle Frank, the husband of Mum's eldest sister, used to work on the railways as a fencer and he played the fiddle 'wondrous gay'. There is the world of difference between a fiddler and a violinist that only those who have heard a fiddler know. When Uncle Frank played the fiddle you wanted to leap and dance and sing and laugh and live.

Out Barmah way where mighty red gums grew, gangs of

sleeper-cutters lived in the bush. Every quarter of the year these men came in to Waaia station to sell their sleepers to the Victorian Railways. A railway inspector came up from Melbourne to examine their red, redolent pile in the station yard. Sometimes the men might have to wait a week, so they camped in the lee of the wheat stacks or up in the big grain shed. Almost to a man they played the gumleaf, getting a variety of tones and pitches from different leaves. They were gregarious and wanted to talk to everyone.

Waaia State School Mothers' Club always had a raffle going for something or other and the day these men got their cheques I'd take my raffle book over and they'd say, 'How much the lot?' and take the whole book between them. I made the transaction last as long as I could because I'd only be permitted to go to their camp this once and it was the only chance I had to watch them work. They used broad axes like the one the executioner used to cut off the head of Mary Queen of Scots, razor-sharp 'trimming' axes to trim the chosen sleepers. The condemned sleepers were sold in the yard, and Dad often could buy them for as little as threepence each. They made the best burning of all and burnt to a hot ash.

We once had a trip to see the sea. Mum, as president of the Mothers' Club, organised this and coaxed Dalton Beswick from the hotel to take us down on his flat-top truck. We travelled all through the night, wrapped in rugs at our mothers' feet while they sat on backless wooden forms. As daylight broke, the truck pulled up and we all climbed stiffly down and stared. As far as our eyes reached there was this shimmering, silver, rippling water. Some of us sifted sand through our fingers but our eyes never left that shimmering mass that rolled over the horizon. At last Billy Wilson broke our trance. 'What a bloody lot of water,' he marvelled.

Aborigines no longer roamed this land although they must have been numerous here once because all the places in the district were named by the blacks before the coming of the white man: Picola, Nathalia, Numurkah, Barmah, Barwoo, and of course

Waaia, which meant water that Aborigines found at Broken Creek. On the New South Wales side of the Murray was the Aboriginal settlement of Cummeragunja where full-bloods and half-castes lived in humpies made of flattened-out kerosene tins. When any of our numerous relatives would visit us we'd take them to this settlement, crossing the Murray on an old cable punt. The men would go fishing along the banks of the river, the women would set up a picnic lunch under the gums, and we kids would play with the Aboriginal children. There were still paddle-steamers on the Murray and the crew and passengers would wave to us as they churned by, and we white kids would try to look as much like blacks as possible by turning our knees in and clasping our hands and putting our heads on the side and giggling shyly as we waved so we too could be thought curios to be examined by the passing parade.

I had a full-blood friend there whose name sounded like Dollery, so I called her Dolly. One night Mum's sister Sadie who played the accordion came up and we had music and singing and dancing on the banks of the Murray in the light of a big fire and the moon, and Dolly sang,

> You may not be an angel,
> But still I'm sure you'll do . . .

and she danced a little behind the fire as the women of her tribe used to do while the men leapt in the forefront of the playabout dancers in the days before we came with our sophistication and weight of numbers. Dolly would sing to me in her language and try to teach me words, but I was not adept and we would roll and giggle helplessly with our arms round each other when I attempted to repeat the lesson. We decided, the two of us, that when she was old enough she would come to work at the Waaia Hotel, as many black girls did, and we would then be close to one another. The Murray has run many a banker since then, and the little black girl who ate bite for bite with me the food I secreted from the packed-away baskets as we sat behind the gums in the dark has no doubt had the sad battle of most of the girls of that place. I hope she remembers that we kissed when we parted at the close of those visits because we were such good friends and only had to look at one another to start laughing. Memory might make clear to her that we are not born with colour prejudice, that she and I did not have it when we were kids together.

Waaia of course had no colour bar. Waaia had no bars of any kind. Black Viney worked at the hotel for a long time and was a good friend of everyone in the town and the boys danced with her at the race ball; we used to ask her to our birthday parties. She went back to Cummeragunja and married a full-blood like herself and came back twelve months later on the train to show us her oily black baby, naked in the heat on a clean white cloth.

'What do you oil him with?' Mum asked as we saw her off in the train.

'Goanna oil, missus,' she replied. Mum wouldn't let us laugh at this, saying that it was a wise precaution to protect the skin against the heat and wind until the child was older. It obviously thrived on whatever she gave it because it was now only weeks old and could sit up and was fat and healthy and laughed the whole time it was awake.

There was plenty of social life for us. Dad had been fond of tennis all his life and here at Waaia he put down a court on the sun-baked red ground and painted lines on it with whitewash and encircled it with wire netting, which also served for the net. Neighbours came from far and near to play on this court, more for the company of lively Dad and the hospitality of Mum than the game. It was too hot to play during the heat of the day; Kevin often came over of a morning and he and I would play from 6 a.m. to 7 a.m., then no one would play until the sun dropped lower around about 6 p.m. From then until night fell the court was never vacant. People arrived in jinkers, on horseback, by push-bike and in tin-lizzies. Mum in mid-summer bought cases of bottled cordials and we kept these in our Coolgardie safe (a wooden frame enclosed by hessian down which water trickled from strips of flannel leading from a dish of water on the top), and when each set finished those four players came in for a drink.

We also had a wireless. Later the Mothers' Club bought one for the school, but ours was the first. In between sets players would come in to listen. *Dad and Dave* was the favourite and our Dad wouldn't miss it – he listened to it for over thirty years and whooped and laughed and identified the characters with men and women he'd known in the bush. Our set had a big speaker like the one in the advertisement for His Master's Voice, and we'd crowd close, turning one ear into this, listening, as much in wonder at hearing anything at all as to attend to the actual broadcast.

Mum was listening intently one day, her ear deep into the flower-like trumpet, and when I walked in she motioned me to be quiet. Then she turned the knob and the machine was silent. She turned to face me and there were tears in her eyes.

'Run over and tell Mrs Young the King is dead,' she said. It was George V.

I delivered the message to Mrs Young, who made the sign of the cross on her forehead and each shoulder, and said, 'May God have mercy on his soul and the souls of all the faithful departed. Amen.'

Then I was to ride to the Tweddles' and tell them the news. This was further away across the wheat fields, far enough for the importance of my mission to manifest itself in me. I was the bearer of tidings of national, nay, world-wide importance. Swiftly but carefully I must go. Marathon, Mercury and Roland the Horse, these names flowed about me. I was little for my age, but now my moment had come. I reached the homestead, dismounted and stalked to the door.

'Madam,' I said to the startled Mrs Tweddle. 'My mother has sent me to inform you that the King is dead. Long live the King!'

For good laughing fun there was nothing to beat a trip to Numurkah on the Casey with Dad on Saturdays. This was a routine trip up and back to see that there was nothing amiss on the section. Mum would give us messages to do in town and money for an ice-cream. Over the loud explosions of the motor Dad would sing,

> One, two, three, Australian boys are we,
> Four, five, six, we've got the Germans in a fix,
> Seven, eight, nine, we'll beat them every time
> There'll be a great time in the old town tonight!

He'd make up rhymes, sometimes as spoken words, sometimes sung to a well-known tune. In between times he'd shout out loud and the birds would shower from the trees in the bush in fright. 'Whacko! Jeanie-weanie-cat's-eyes!' because my eyes are green. And, 'We'll cut old Mickie's head off 'cause she doesn't want it on' – this was a cry from the old Stiffy and Mo days, seemingly.

It's only an old piece of bunting, it's only an old coloured rag,
But many have died for its honour, and shed their life's blood for the flag.

His favourites were quotations, of which he knew hundreds, but the two most frequently used by him were,

> Life is mostly froth and bubble, two things stand like stone,
> Kindness in another's trouble, courage in your own.

and:

> Lives of great men all remind us, we must make our lives sublime,
> And in passing leave behind us footprints on the sands of time.

We'd always have a dog with us, sometimes two dogs. Nip we'd had since I was a toddler. He was supposed to be mine, but he deserted me as soon as he met Dad and never left his side until his own death of old age. Nip was a great rabbiter and as the Casey roared on he would sit, nose into the wind, watching for the bob of a white tail ahead. Then he'd whine and paw at Dad to pull up so he could range out across the plain in pursuit.

Even better on rabbits than Nip was Whacko. This dog was given to me by a schoolteacher who bred water spaniels. I'd heard him tell the bigger boys, 'A nigger got in the wood-pile this time.' Whacko was one of the results. An odder dog never took to the bush. He was big-boned, ugly as sin, with a tail like a kangaroo that he swung wildly from side to side in excessive exuberance and joy of life. If you were walloped round the legs by this two-foot-long tail like a piece of rubber piping you really felt it. There were times when tears sprang to my eyes as he lovingly walloped me. The day I carried him home as a puppy Dad was waiting for me. I put him on the ground to show him off and Dad took one look and said, 'Whacko!' and laughed. The name stuck. I lost the pup, for no dog could resist Dad. He jumped off the Casey when it was going full speed once and broke his leg. The men brought him home on a bag and set the leg in splints, and though he could only use it thereafter as a balance he nevertheless was just as good a rabbiter and once ran down a hare on his three good legs and the brummy one.

Waaia was not rich in bird life because of the scarcity of trees and water, but we learnt to call those we knew up to us. Alex Walker, now known throughout Australia as the 'Birdman', taught us. Alex was an odd-job man. He was a cross-country rider, boot-mender and wheat-lumper – he'd have a go at anything – but his great love was birds. He trained our school (fourteen on the roll at that time) to whistle and call curlews, cockatoos, crows, magpies, pallid cuckoos, kookaburras and many others, and then he took us down to Shepparton radio station where we went on the air.

The parents all piled into our house back at Waaia to listen in while we first sang 'Bird of the Wilderness', and then went into our repertoire.

'Jean Smith,' said the announcer, 'will now imitate the pallid cuckoo and the blackbird.' Kevin with the morepork followed. Oh, we were big time that night, all right!

School concerts were another opportunity for us to show off. I always gave lots of items, not because I was a better performer than the others but because the teacher knew he could depend on Mum to dress me well. If it were a toss-up between a new dress for herself or a stage costume for me Mum didn't hesitate. I was a jester in crimson and gold, a pied piper in red and yellow, a 'sweet queen of loveliness and grace' in blue brocade, and Ted Jorgenson sang to me 'Dressed in your gown of blue brocade', and we trod a measure or two of a minuet. We thought it was all very aesthetic.

Weddings were fun, or at least our part in them, which seems in retrospect to have been restricted to kitchen teas and tin kettlings. Kitchen teas were a good excuse for a dance. Everyone brought gifts and placed them on a table near the stage – you didn't have to know the parties concerned, everyone was welcome. Bill Leaf always made a speech and the prospective groom would reply. Tin kettlings came after the bride and groom settled in their home, usually the day of the wedding in those times when honeymoons couldn't be afforded.

When Bill Martin and Bessie Leaf were married I made as much noise as anyone with my old saucepan and soup ladle. We drove up to within half a mile of their house and walked the rest of the way, creeping silently on foot to surprise the couple. We surrounded the house and at a signal began to bang our 'kettles'. Some did have kettles, others had pots, pans, dishes, iron bars, bolts, crank handles, anything that would make a noise. All round the house we stood, banging and singing 'For they are jolly good fellows' until they opened the door and let us in. Then everyone threw their 'kettles' on the roof – except the man who had an enamel bedroom utensil which he placed decoratively on the roof of the front porch – and trooped inside. Bessie had a baby grand piano (the first time I'd seen this it was in her father's house and it so filled the front room one had to sidle in past it). There was enough space around it in her new home for us all to dance around it as she played. After supper we sang 'We won't go home till morning', and the adults made sly remarks which we children didn't understand but pretended we did.

Travelling shows were few and far between. Times were hard. A man once came to the school and wrote out by hand a note for each of us to take home. This said he would perform 'tricks of magic and entertainment' in the hall the following day and the teacher was willing to let the pupils off early from school. The charge would be a penny for children, threepence for adults. Somehow the parents of all of us read this to mean it was a children's show only and therefore didn't come . . . and the best stage magician I have ever seen played to fourteen children and Mr Gregory our teacher for 1s 5d.

I was first to bring home news of another travelling show. I found it one morning when I was bringing the cows home. We would put our cows up the line at night to graze, and in the morning I'd go after them on the pull-trike. This was my favourite lone expedition. In the crisp, early morning air I'd go off with an apple or sandwich, take the trike from the shed and turn it on the line, and off I'd set pulling the handle in, out, in, out, for a mile up to the crossing towards Numurkah. There I'd let the rails down in the fence and our cows would cross the road to our side of the crossing. Then they would plod home without any help from me, anxious as they were to have their udders relieved. At the crossing I must turn the trike around to face home. It was a heavy, solid thing with three big iron wheels. An unskilled grown man would have found difficulty turning such a machine. I, with one hand doing the 'lifting', which was more like swinging, and with the other hand steadying, with my apple held casually in my mouth, was nonchalantly turning this thing of wood and iron on the rails one morning when a man and woman appeared. They found this sight of a very small girl effortlessly turning such a weight so interesting they asked me to their camp for a cup of tea.

'Who taught you to do that?' the woman asked me.

'My mother. She can do anything.' As I said this, the man turned a somersault without putting hand to the ground.

'Can your mother do this?'

I was too amazed to think of the humour of dear roly-poly

Mum doing a free-flip.

They were camped in a clump of trees in a caravan drawn by two mules.

'We are entertainers. You must come to see us.'

I had half Waaia waiting for them by the time they trundled in and put on their show that night outside the hall, with lanterns hung on forked sticks for illumination. They were a bright pair. The man played the violin all ways – behind his back, above his head, between his legs, with a bow and with a broomstick. The woman sang and clacked castanets, and the mules did odd tricks and were dressed for one item as famous figures. It was a good show, fast-moving and funny, but Waaia itself put on the best act when the front seat collapsed and all the young girls including Mickie and her friends the Martin twins, Rene and Anne, went head over heels backwards.

'What a poppy show!' the boys said at school next day.

THE
OPEN ROAD

imes being what they were there were many swaggies on
the roads: a strange, wandering race who played life solo.
They all had serenity, and I sometimes wonder if the times
didn't give them the excuse to find solitude and freedom from
conformity.

Waaia was on the time-honoured trade route of swagmen
coming down through central New South Wales. They had some
kind of bush telegraph or perhaps secret signs like gipsies, because
they made straight for our place, passing others by without a
glance. Mum was always good for a handout.

'Would you mind fillin' me billy, missus?' they would ask,
and hand a blackened billy and cotton bag of tea over. Mum
would never use their tea.

'These times none of us know who'll be next on the track,' she would say. Always she'd give a man 'on the wallaby' a few cuts off the roast, some vegetables and fruit and a slab of cake. If it was near our mealtime she'd tell him to leave his tin plate and later Dad would take his meal up. These men always camped in the lee of the wheat shed and when Dad went with the meal I went with him.

'A bit of scran, mate,' Dad would say. Dad never spoke much, but seemed more like a receptacle for other people's thoughts. I heard more telling, interesting, pungent comments made to Dad than anyone else. These men would usually talk of the track, tell of mates 'crook' who had to be left behind (a swagman wasn't allowed to stay more than forty-eight hours in one town), of 'hard runs' where the squatters 'turned their mongs on a man'. Some were well spoken, some were dead-beats. Some were old, some young, some garrulous, some taciturn, but I never heard one of them speak of his background. Who they were, where they came from and who they left behind we never knew. None of those who came to our house were 'bots'. While Mum was boiling the water for their billy they would go over to the woodheap, unasked, and cut a pile of wood, or stack what Dad had cut. One man used to sell clothes pegs made from willows, another made dippers from old 7-pound treacle tins using the lids to make firm handles. Until the end of her life Mum used one of these solid, craftsmanlike utensils, the solder smooth and almost invisible. This same man used to make 'jardinières' with curled and twisted ornamentation and legs, tastefully painted. Mickie had one for years.

The swagmen's rig-out was uniform and consisted of things that could be found in any country home, as Sylvia Martin and I found the day we became swaggies too.

Mum had gone away for the day and I had known in advance that she would, so we planned well ahead. When Dad left for work we were to meet at the big gum down in our house paddock where the swaggies often rested.

I found most of my 'clobber' in the wash-house – an old pair of dungaree trousers and an old 'bluey', a bushman's coat. I tied a pair of raw-hide bowyangs round my trousers below the knees to stop them dragging with the weight of wet mud in winter (it was now actually the heart of summer and we were in the midst of dry, crackling drought). The hat position was difficult. There was a wonderful battered felt under the bath, but I couldn't get my hair up under it so I settled for Dad's old cloth cap instead. Mick helped me pack a swag with spare clothes and roll a bluey from an old grey blanket. This I tied across the front of my chest and around my back. I had a billy to carry in my hand and a frying pan to tie on my swag. Mick gave me a clean washed flour-bag with tea and another with sugar. I had gathered bottles and old newspapers to sell at the store in exchange for bacon and bread.

Then I was off. I was a little late and found it hard to keep my steps languid and unhurried as I ran out the gate and looked down for Sylvia, who should be there by now. She wasn't. Instead, to my alarm, a real swaggie was sitting under the tree, resting his back on its trunk and rolling a cigarette. As I approached he lit up and rolled over on his side, surveying my coming. I had to pass him to get out of the far end of the paddock to go and look for Sylvia. He didn't take his eyes off me. I skipped along a bit and then tried to look nonchalant like a real swaggie, but it was hard what with my trousers falling down and my hair pushing my cap off my head, and me trying to rectify matters by holding my trousers up with my elbows and wondering whether to drop the billy so I could tuck my hair in again. I wished I could have worn a hat like this real swaggie. His felt hat had strings with corks on the ends hanging down all round the brim to keep the flies off his face. I was almost opposite him when I heard Sylvia's voice. The swaggie was she.

'I thought you were a real swaggie,' I told her. 'Can you smoke?'

'Yes, can't you?'

'Of course.' I wouldn't do less than her. She handed me the makings. It was like canary seed and I couldn't keep it in the paper. Finally I got a sort of rough cigarette made, lit it and drew in. It was wonderful. I drew in again and let the smoke trail through my nostrils. Then I wondered how I'd ever get enough of them – they were so good. I smoked four more before the day was out and didn't change my opinion of them. There by the tree I hitched up my trousers and took the ribbon off the top of my hair, which made the cap sit down better.

Over at the store we handed over our bottles and papers and while we were waiting for Mr Fowler, the shop assistant, who was the father of our friend Dorothy, to weigh up our bacon, the manager, who had been playing cards at our house the night before, came by, looked at us, then said, 'You want to give the gentlemen of the open road a fair crack of the whip, Bill. It's a hard row they hoe.' We were very pleased to have this proof of the success of our impersonation. With the 1s 1½d we were given we bought bacon, two chocolate bars and two penny aniseed balls that would last all day.

For a while we squatted beside the railway gates watching the wheat wagons go by, and then we set off to light a fire and boil our billy. Mr Tweddle, the wheat-farmer, came down as we were about to begin our meal. We heard him coming, galloping hell for leather down the side of his paddock of ripe wheat, heading for where we had our fire blazing beside the dam.

'Hey! You!' he yelled when he was still at a distance. We stood up. He reined in his horse a little then and broke down to a canter, shading his eyes to see us the better. When he came up to us he said, 'Well, well, and how are you two blokes going, eh?' Perspiration was running down his face and he took out a handkerchief and mopped it off. 'You gave me one devil of a scare when I saw that fire going so close to the wheat. You know how it is, one spark and the whole crop would go, ripe and dry as it is.' We began to worry. Our faces must have shown this. Mr Tweddle quickly went on, 'But of course I didn't know it was two old hands at the game down here. It could have been two new-chums who didn't know how to take care of a fire in these parts.' We cheered a little at this further proof of the effectiveness of our disguise.

'But you two – I'd stake my life on it that you were just going to carry water from the dam now your billy's boiling. You were going to put your fire out.'

'Oh yes,' we said. 'That's what we were going to do.' We doused the fire.

As Mr Tweddle rode away he called back to us, 'Good luck and a dry bed, mates,' and waved his whip to us.

We looked with glee at one another. He didn't know us either! No one recognised us! When the goods train came in we walked over to the station and asked the engine-driver for some hot water for our billy.

'It's not safe to light a fire in these parts,' we told him solemnly.

While we were walking back to the goods shed to brew our tea we passed the guard, who was uncoupling wheat trucks. Out of habit I grabbed the hose-like coupling as it swung free and, putting it to my lips, spoke into it as into a telephone. Sylvia dropped her swag and capered up to the other end of the truck and did likewise. The guard stopped his work to look at us. Realising this was hardly in character we dropped the toy and shambled off as swaggies do, sure that our momentary lapse was not enough to give the game away.

I didn't ask till I was much older who had told on us. Someone certainly had. A week after our adventure Mum waited for me with the razor strop when I came in from school. (The engine-driver it was, laughingly telling of the great amusement caused all round by a little girl dressed up as a swagman, unaware that he was getting me the strop.)

16

THE SWAMPLANDS

O f course we didn't stay at Waaia too long. After two years Mum had itchy feet.

'You want to get on the wallaby, Birdie?' Dad asked. 'Is there anything going?' There was never any difficulty in getting a transfer. The foot-loose fettler and the station-master with wanderlust moved from one area to another and 'the Heads' knew they took with them new methods of work and, as well, injected an impetus and social vigour into isolated outposts stagnating in the wet blanket of the Depression.

In his work the railwayman built up a tradition of service that only he and his immediate community knew of. It was a tradition that was born of a complete sense of being part of a great movement. 'The Great Family of Railway Workers'

Harold Clapp called them (and they, in their turn, called him the greatest transport man Australia had known).

'Is there anything going?'

There was a small caretaker-and-fettler station vacancy in Gippsland and within three weeks we were there. Waaia put on a farewell for us at the hall and old Bill Leaf made a speech and had a final waltz with me, and Mum and Dad were presented with a travelling rug. It didn't seem real to be leaving. Other places were different; Waaia was truly home. I think all of us there knew we'd surely be back.

Monomeith was in the Kooweerup swamplands, a flat area cut across by canals that drained the former wastelands of their water. Now it was a lush dairying land, although there were patches, such as one near our house, of rank swamp left where snakes abounded. Nip enjoyed this. He was a great snake-catcher and rarely a week went by that he didn't bring one home.

Monomeith had no pub, no shop, nothing but us. The railway station was post office too, as it had been at Nowingi. There were several big properties nearby. The nearest was Paddy Einsedel's racing stud. Here the old man, who raised such stake-winners as Waltzing Lily and Black Alec, had a station-homestead type of establishment and a big garage in which he had three cars, two stuffed crocodiles, snakes in bottles, hundreds of odd exhibits, and many etchings and cartoons. It was one of the finest private bizarre museums.

This line was a busy one, but not many of the trains stopped at our station; most of them went to the coal town of Wonthaggi direct, not stopping at any of the little stations in between. Our house was up on the platform itself and in the nights when you were in bed you could feel the crunch, crunch, crunch of the passing trains like nailed boots walking across your bedroom floor. I soon learnt to distinguish full trucks from empty ones, and the different kinds of wagons, coal trucks, cattle trucks and passenger coaches.

'There was something wrong with the early train going up

this morning,' I told my father at breakfast one day. 'It seemed unfinished.'

That night Dad told me he had spoken to the driver on his return trip and told him what I'd said.

'We'd coupled a flat-top behind the guard's van to shunt off at Caldermeade,' the driver had said. 'Therefore she couldn't "get" the van and the train would sound incomplete.' I certainly knew my trains.

Sometimes a train would pull up and shunt trucks into our siding; then you would see tarpaulins lift and heads pop out while men 'jumping the rattler' looking for work tried to get their bearings. If they saw us kids looking they'd put their fingers to their lips conspiratorially and disappear back under the tarp. Dad knew we knew of this illegal traffic. He said, 'Try not to see it, but try not to forget it when you have full and plenty.'

One day the train pulled up and they weren't shunting. Lying awake in my bed I couldn't work out what they were doing. I got up and looked out the window. A man was walking along the platform forcing the guard to undo the lashings holding the tarps down. He was after the illegal passengers, but as fast as he climbed in one side of a truck men sprang over the other side and sprinted into the low, wet, swampy scrub and disappeared. The guard did no more than he was ordered to do by the 'head'. I thought at first that the men were negroes: they were all black from travelling in the coal trucks.

Suddenly one of the men was trapped. He hadn't been able to squeeze out the other side and had jumped onto the platform. The 'head' had his back to him trying to hustle the guard in his task. The guard looked up and saw the man as he jumped. He would be unable to get away because the gates to this platform were locked each night. The guard quickly motioned with his head towards our house gate and as he looked up saw my face at the window. The man ran in the gate through our rose garden and round the back of the house. When the 'head' gave up and went back to the van, the guard motioned me to put the window up.

'Tell your dad,' he said softly, nodding towards the back of the house.

At Monomeith I went to school by train each day to the next 'town', Caldermeade, travelling free in the guard's van. This day I was told by the guard that I was to travel in the passenger coach, and as I stepped in I saw a figure bolt from our gate into the van. He looked like Dad; he was dressed in clothes very like Dad's old suit, which I never saw after that day . . . Strange times when a man who could have been one's own father was on the run because he'd committed the crime of not being able to find a job.

On Melbourne Cup day the gang would work near the station so they could listen to the broadcast of the great race. On our first Cup day at Monomeith the goods train pulled in just before 3 p.m. and the driver, seeing the trikes pulled off the side of the track, came in to listen too, beckoning the guard after him. Dad saw a tarpaulin on a truck lift up a little so he opened the windows and the door wide and turned the great trumpet towards the train to enable the men on the 'rattler' to hear too.

When we first moved to Monomeith we went to school there, a tiny square room a mile from our place. It had a total of eight pupils when Mick and I were mustered. It had survived only because the Railways Department had told the Education Department they were going to send a couple with children to the station. Mickie was sixteen and didn't want to go to school. One day as we got to the school gate she just went on walking.

'Don't say anything to anyone till tonight,' she warned me. All day I sweated it out. When I got home at 4 p.m. after giving her seven hours' start Mum said, 'Where's your sister?'

'Walking.'

Mum had to move quickly. She didn't know what Mick had in mind except she did know that she hated school. Mum, who I'd seen meet many a crisis calmly, tried to meet this one in the same way, but she was bewildered and tears welled in her eyes. Then the phone rang. Mick had turned up at Auntie May's farm eleven miles away at Nar Nar Goon.

This had the effect of ending Mick's school days, which was what Mick intended, but it also ended Monomeith school's days, for now, with only seven pupils, the school had to close. I would travel to Caldermeade station by train then walk a mile along the road to Caldermeade school between sweet hedges of may. At night I must walk all the way home for there was no suitable train, but sometimes as I'd plod along beside the 'five-foot' gauge an unscheduled goods train would pull up and I'd be hauled up on the footplate or into the guard's van and given the run of the crib tins while we rattled homewards. On one memorable occasion the Commissioner's car actually pulled up and took me home. This vehicle was an ordinary car with the rubber tyres replaced by flanged steel wheels and with the steering wheel removed. It was used by 'heads' only. It gave Mum, as she later declared, 'quite a turn' to see the Commissioner's car pulling up unexpectedly at her station and then to see Harold Clapp himself handing her child up onto the platform.

Smoothing down her starched apron with the Dolly Varden needlework she watched the Dodge disappear. 'You didn't say *anything* did you . . .' – not really a question; she knew her daughter too well to think she would keep quiet if asked to speak. It was more like a cry from the dark depths of her being. 'You didn't say anything!' Oh no, I assured her, I'd said nothing. It was Mr Clapp and the other gentlemen who talked, and when I answered it seemed to delight them so I carried on, making quite an impression on them. They laughed and laughed. They even asked the chauffeur to slow down the motor so we would have more time to talk and he laughed too.

'Do you still go to Mass on the Casey as you did at Waaia?'

'Oh no! We don't have Caseys here.' I lectured the Commissioners on the reasons why we didn't have a motor.

'We have pull-trikes here so we can hear the trains coming. But there aren't many trains on Sundays.' And what about Saturday night outings? Surely we visit the other railway families along the line? 'All railway families visit on Saturday night,' His Nibs said to me.

'Oh yes, but we take the quad then, not the pull-quad but the pump-quad with the iron bars like crowbars to pump the wheels with, and do you know we had an awful accident last Saturday night and Mum says those jolly things shouldn't be allowed and were enough to kill a body.' Mr Clapp said, 'Really! Are they?'

'Oh yes. Mum and Dad were standing up pushing the iron bars up and down and Mick – she's my sister . . .'

'Yes,' said Mr Clapp. 'I remember Mick.'

'Well, we were sitting on the flat-quad and someone, Mum says it wasn't her, put the bar into the wheel-turning-slot at the wrong time and over we went.'

'Where? Over where?'

'Over the bridge. Down into the canal. Of course it's dry now in summer.'

'Was anyone hurt?'

'Yes, Mum was sort of unconscious for a while and then Dad got her and us kids back up onto the bridge and we all lifted the trike – by Jove those quads are heavy blooming things [Dad's words] – back onto the line and off we went to Caldermeade to the Yates's to play crib.'

'And Mrs Yates looked after your mother?'

'Oh no. We couldn't tell them what happened because there were strangers there and we never talk railway business to outsiders.' Yes, I let him know I knew our duty as a railway family.

'May all the saints in heaven help us,' cried Mum, looking up to the sky for a sign.

When Dad came home he said it didn't matter. 'There is a saying among railwaymen that the man who hasn't broken a rule is the man out looking for a job.' Mr Clapp knew this, Dad said, like any good employer would. 'He knows we work hard and well and we're loyal.'

That was my first experience of going over a bridge. I soon repeated it. We used to walk two miles in the other direction to Kooweerup to Mass, and one Sunday coming home, when

Mick and I were well ahead of our parents, I showed off, demonstrating how I could walk the parapet of a bridge.

'Garn!' said Mick. 'That's nothing. I bet you can't run.'

As I opened my eyes I could dimly see Mick bending over me. One leg was twisted strangely beneath me and my thumb hung at right angles to my hand. Mick dragged me from the canal bed up onto the railway track, but I couldn't get my left foot to the ground. It was many months before I walked on it again and some years before I got out of the boots needed to strengthen the ankle. For much of the damage old Dr Appleford at Lang Lang blamed the liberal application of iodine my mother had put on.

'Iodine has caused more crippled children than any other common medical aid in this country,' the old man said. At that time iodine was considered almost a cure-all by bush people.

'It prevents the bruise coming out,' the doctor said. To counteract this he ordered that my foot remain higher than my hip until the bruise did come out. This was very trying. For a week the leg looked pasty, then it looked a little puffed-up and blue. Within a month the whole leg from toe to hip was mottled blue-purple-black, and I'd gaze at it in wonder propped up beside me as I practised the piano.

I was studying for a music exam and when the time came Mum carried me from the train in Melbourne to the tram and from there into the Conservatorium. In those months she carried me many miles, and I was no longer small for my age; instead I was a fat, roly-poly child. Once she carried me two miles to have me inoculated against diphtheria.

I was still unable to walk, but I could get my foot to the ground when the great floods of 1936 came to the Gippsland swamplands. All day, all night and all the next day and night the rain emptied out onto the swamps. The canals were running a banker. Then disaster came. The canals carrying water out to the sea met with a high tide coming in, and back over the land ran the water carrying the canal banks with it. Many people in Gippsland swear to this day it was a tidal wave; they had never seen the tide so high.

On that second night of rain, just after we had gone to bed, there came a knocking on our front door.

'Albert! The canal's giving way. Come and lend a hand.' This was the canal nearest to us. Dad didn't come home for four days. All night they battled, lugged sand-bags and shovelled up rubble into holes in the banks. Then, led by their ganger, the gang went in to give a hand to the people who were trapped in their homes.

At home we were perfectly safe because of the house being off the ground up on the platform. We always had good stocks of food in our cupboards. On the second day Mum heard on the radio that homeless people were being brought in to the railway station at Kooweerup. She walked in to help. Where she walked on the five-foot gauge the swirling waters lapped over her shoes, the ballast had been swept away and the sleepers were held up only because they were fastened to the rails. The whole line in parts was swinging. Crossing the bridge over which I had fallen to the canal below when it was dry she was ankle-deep in water. As she paddled along from sleeper to sleeper down the track where it crosses the main street of Kooweerup she waved to friends of ours who were rowing up the main street after being rescued from their roof-tops.

Dad and the other fettlers brought in scores of people who had been cut off on high ground or in the ceilings of their homes. At one house where the owners had desperately tried to protect their home by sealing up the windows and doors the whole house was spinning round in the raging waters. The water had run over the land so suddenly that most people were taken unawares. The Bush Nursing Hospital was caught this way. The fettlers cut through the roof of that building to take out the patients, several of whom were elderly and in a state of shock. Mum, helping patients out of the boat when it reached the Kooweerup station, found Dad's coat round an old lady who had only a thin nightdress beneath it; an old man had lost his pyjamas and was wrapped in a blanket. The gang carried several people into the waiting room, now being used as a first-aid post.

Back at home Mick and I were enjoying every moment. A Tiger Moth plane had flown over, quite low! We had seen a photographer lean out! We were in the news!

The land at the back of our house fell away so sharply that our back yard was actually sixteen feet lower than our rose garden. When the floods came, Mum opened the gates and let our animals in. We had six cows and now they climbed up and made themselves at home near our wash-house. Each time we went to the lavatory we had to move a milking cow out of the way. The poultry came up here too; roosters, hens, chickens and ducks perched in the shrubs and on the rose bushes. The Victorian Railways gave an annual award for the best garden at a fettler's home and this rose garden had won the prize two years running. Now it looked indescribably funny with poor bedraggled hens skulking among the buds and roosters with their wet tail feathers dangling in the Cecil Brunner archway.

Without a break for a rest when the danger had passed the gang must get the line ready for trains to resume. Mrs Yates, the station-mistress from Caldermeade, and her husband came down on their trike and we set off with ours to survey the damage. We got as far as the bridge I had fallen over. It was too dangerous to take the pull-trikes further than that on the swinging rails, so I stayed there with my gammy leg and the others walked on, the men prodding with long sticks and noting rails twisted and bent.

There was a hillock near me which was all that was left of a canal bank, and it was moving with living things. Snakes, lizards and rabbits were there, all cheek by jowl, their ancient feuds forgotten in their common fear. Then I screamed. A snake was swimmng directly for the line, its head cocked up like a periscope. Old Nip came bounding back to me, jumping from sleeper to sleeper, leant out over the water and neatly bit its head off. The snake threshed for a moment then sank beneath the muddy waste. Nip began to look for more amusement of a similar kind and scampered round barking happily as he peered into the water where eddies and floating sticks deceived him. The Yateses had a dog, a small thing, a 'snivelling lap dog' as Dad would have called it had it belonged to anyone other than a friend. This fool dog became excited at Nip's barking and fell into the water and disappeared immediately.

I called for the adults and they formed a chain with Dad out at the extreme end, shoulder deep in the moving water. He leant down to where the wire fence should be and caught hold of the little dog and dragged it free. Almost as soon as it hit the air it was sick and began its infernal yapping again.

A lavatory sailed by on its back, the door hanging off its hinges as it circled ponderously in the current.

'Look at the dike,' Dad called. We laughed. After it floated a small box like a miniature of the privy.

'It's a toy,' I told Dad. 'I know!' Dad waded out after it – after all, he could get no wetter than he was – and brought it in. It was a toy sewing machine and he oiled and cleaned it for me and it went for years.

I was spoilt. I had everything. Mick had everything she wanted too, but she was not conceited. I was because I considered I had more than she had, and what is more that I was entitled to more because I had Mum and Dad. Although no one ever mentioned it and she and I were treated the same as one another, I thought of it often. They were mine. I thought poor, poor Mickie.

Of course she did have brothers. Jack and Bob came to visit us at Monomeith. Jack was in an orphanage. He had been in one orphanage or another since his father died all those years ago. He had no conception of life as lived by people in ordinary homes, nor did he know anything of worldly things. He told us, with the cruelty of youth, of the hardships of the orphanage where a handful of nuns cared for 150 abandoned children.

'Those nuns are mean. When they take us to town they only give us threepence each to spend.'

Mum wondered aloud how much scraping the nuns had to do to give that treat to all those children in those times.

Bob was better off. He also was in an orphanage, but during

112

the school holiday periods he could earn his keep on the farm of the people who owned the property where his father had pitched his tent before the family broke up. Thus Bob had a base. Though the boys and Mickie hadn't been together since they were infants they fell into the warp and weft of each other's lives. Bob was friendly to me, Jack loved me, but Mick was their sister.

'Blood is thicker than water,' Mum consoled me. Yes, I thought then, that is how it should be. How few years were to pass before I knew how false that old wives' tale was. How few years before Mum was to repeat that remark so fearfully.

As Christmas neared I alone waited for Santa Claus. The others were too old for such things, they said. I, too, was too old, but I was reluctant to give up this last link with the world of make-believe, and the rest of the family encouraged me to hang up my stocking for the last time.

One night from my bed I heard Paddy Einsedel talking to Mum and Dad in the lounge while they played cards. Old Paddy was saying what a good rider I was.

'I've got a nice little horse that would suit her ladyship,' he said. 'I'll give it to you for her Santa Claus.'

I rolled over. I had heard enough. A horse of my own! When Christmas morning dawned I followed the string tied to the head of my bed. Everyone tagged along behind me: Dad, Mum, Mick and her two brothers. Round the house the string went and round the house we pursued it, through the rose garden, over the buddleia bush and then out the back gate where it ended . . . tied to the handle-bars of a shiny new bicycle. They all waited for my cry of joy. I untied the string, turned the bike to face downhill, gave it a push and ran inside the house. My horse, my lovely, moving, shining, living, striding horse. I wouldn't cry, I wouldn't let them see me cry. Never would they see me cry. I waited an hour, but no one came.

God, then I did cry. Mum and Dad were hard pressed for money. They'd helped too many people, pay was £4 a week. Mick and I were the best fed and the best dressed at every school we went to. Where had they got the money for it? I knew how they were struggling to keep payments up on the piano. The bike must have been purchased the same way. For me. And then – Oh God, I wanted to go to them, but I couldn't. The weight on my heart was hurting me. The pain would ease if I went to them. If our arms were round one another it would go. They knew me and loved me and would forgive me. But I couldn't go; I didn't go.

Mick came in to get ready for church. She said she hated me.

'I don't bloody well care,' I said. She hit me hard for that, across the head.

I felt better. 'Bloody, hell, damn.'

Jack crept in. He'd brought the bike back. 'There's not a mark on it. Come and I'll teach you to ride.'

'Can you ride?' I asked him.

'No, but I'll learn. I'll get a bike when I get a job. Yes, I'll get a job and I'll live here and you and I will ride into Kooweerup to the pictures.' And so it happened that Mum was mother to one more.

'Come and look at us!' Jack would yell to Mum and Dad, knowing it was what I wanted to yell. Then we'd show off, he and I. One-leg riding, no-leg riding with both feet on the handle-bars, duo riding with arms round each other's shoulders; then we'd ride hell for leather to within a yard of my parents and spring off backwards from the seat bringing the bike to a standstill. Hey! And I wouldn't look at Mum's eyes because I knew that they'd tell me that she had forgiven me.

I was at the 'awkward age', an aptly named period of clumsy manoeuvres more of the mind than the body, an urgent awareness of the world and everything in it coupled with an inability to articulate. Paddy Einsedel the horse-breeder was one of the few people who could approach a child at that age as an equal, on a level of comprehension. One Saturday I watched him leaving for the races at Caulfield. I had saved two shillings to spend on our annual holiday.

'Give it to me and I'll win you a ten bob note,' he suggested.

I handed it over immediately and that night when he got off the train he handed me a ten shilling note and my own two shillings back. Waltzing Lily had come home at five to one.

Paddy named his horses after people who worked for him. His best filly, Waltzing Lily, was named after Lily Walters, his housemaid. One night the housekeeper had caught Lily creeping in late from a dance and in the morning hauled her in front of Paddy.

'What were you doing to that hour?' he asked.

'Waltzing,' answered the girl.

'Waltzing,' the old man said with a reminiscent smile. 'Waltzing Lily.' When the next filly was born its name was registered as just that. Bicycle Nelly was named after Lily's sister, who used to ride home to Nar Nar Goon each weekend; Black Alec, the great colt, after Alec the chauffeur, who appeared one day covered in grease.

There was little in the way of entertainment at this place, certainly none of the social life Waaia had. Because of this I looked forward to Anzac Day when, as the teacher at school had told us, there would be some kind of celebration. We could, if we were permitted, wear our fathers' ribbons and war medals. The engine-driver nodded his head in approval that morning as I crossed the platform to the guard's van with the medals clanking on their long, vivid ribbons across my breast.

We were taken by truck from the school to the Lang Lang hall for a combined school service.

This was the type of dramatic group I liked. We sang the Recessional and said the Lord's Prayer. A town councillor made a long speech about what we owed to the soldiers who lay in Flanders fields, but we noticed he didn't have any medals, and then another man told us about men going to fight for God, King and country and he didn't have any medals either.

There was another man sitting on the platform with the officials, but they didn't ask him to speak so he pushed forward and spoke without being asked. He didn't have any medals. He didn't need any to show that he had been there. He had a hook where his hand used to be. He told us about the morning they leapt into the water before the dawn came up and waded in holding their rifles above their heads. He was nervous when he began, but as we sat quietly listening, wading, falling, struggling, seeing men die with him on that grey, explosive, violent morning, he gained poise.

He hadn't liked what the previous speakers had said about men fighting for God, King and country.

'I didn't think of God, King and country when I enlisted,' he said. 'I was seventeen years old. Any boy who can hear a military band and not fall in behind it might live a long time but he won't have much fun.'

He spoke simply, with no heroics, and used the great Australian adjective whenever he became distressed. He made that nation-crowning day leap out of the past and claim us. That day I looked for a second on Gallipoli, and patriotism stirred in me for the first time. I felt the reputation haloed about us that the deaths of these men and the buoyancy of their spirit had earned, a reputation that every Australian from that day on has been born with as his inheritance. Tears coursed down my cheeks as they have often coursed since that day, tears not of sorrow but of pride.

At home Mum thrashed me and made me promise to confess my sin to the priest. I had been to a Protestant ceremony. I was a devout Catholic. The only literature I'd been permitted since I'd learnt to read was the catechism. I knew it by heart. Now I rebelled. I told the priest what I had done, but I added that had I known what the ceremony was I would still have gone.

17

HOMETOWN

Then we were on the wallaby again. Mum and Dad pored over the *Gazette* every time it arrived and laconically discussed the vacancies. Then one issue had the place we were all looking for: Waaia station was 'up' again.

Waaia welcomed us back with sunshine and many friends waiting on the platform for our train to arrive.

Dad said to the gang assembled to meet him, 'Well, I'm back.'

'About time,' they said to him.

There was a thin, nasty woman schoolteacher now, but even she couldn't spoil that school. Ted Jorgenson and Alan Thornton were ready for me.

'Are you as stupid as ever?' they wanted to know. We were all in grade seven now.

There was a mice plague in the district; we had never experienced one before. In a brief silence during our first meal we heard a whispering, as though the wind were stirring through the wheat crops. We went outside and listened. There was no wind. We walked out to the crop beyond our gate. There, running through the dry, golden stalks was a movement of brown as a million mice ran in battalions. It was awesome. We went back inside the house, afraid of what might meet us there. As it turned out we were little troubled by comparison with others. Our house was built behind the station platform, and the mice not being able to climb this hillock ran round it from their breeding places in the wheat stacks and converged well behind our house in the crops. We set traps, single, double and multiple types with four, six and even eight holes round the circular trap, and when the plague had ended we had only caught a hundred or so. The station also missed out, only a few documents in a seldom-used cupboard being eaten.

Some people got a real going-over. The Marvels in particular.

'We can't complain,' we raced home and told Mum after our first visit to the Marvels on our return. 'Mice chew the hard parts off the feet of the Marvels while they sleep.'

It was true. They showed us their feet, under the ball and heel particularly where hard calluses had grown because of going without shoes and never washing. The mice had nibbled deep until they bit raw flesh and wakened the sleepers.

'I fixed them,' big 'Bull' Marvel told us. 'I set a trap.'

This trap consisted of a kerosene tin a quarter full of water. On the top edge of this balanced a stick with a piece of cheese on the end of it, and when the mice ran out to the cheese the stick fell into the water taking the mice with it.

'Some mornings the tin is half full,' Bull told us with pride.

Over at the wheat stacks the damage was enormous. A mouse had only to nibble a hole in one bag to bring a whole stack down. What used to be a skyline of symmetrical blocks was now a drunken wave of collapsed stacks. Fires were smouldering all day beside the stacks burning the torn bags and dead mice.

Nip and Whacko had a great time and never tired of pouncing playfully on the tiny creatures, but our cat after a few days of gluttony rarely bothered to cross the line.

One Saturday Kevin and I made two shillings each. A wheat-buyer offered us this amount for a kerosene tin full of mice. Using a rubber-ended fly-swat we raced round thwacking the teeming things near a badly drilled wheat stack. It took a hard thwack to stun them, but once in the tin they couldn't escape. When our tins were a quarter full we covered the mice with water and later tipped the lot into the middle of the fire. We tore round squealing and yelling and slipping over the wheat that lay in sour yellow piles where it had spilled from the bags. Instead of the clean, ripe smell of the fields it was now musty and sickening.

For hours we danced about whacking without mercy. The only time we'd desist was when we came on a nest, and then we'd wait, sitting down to watch, while the frantic mother carried each of the naked, blind babies away to another dark hiding place.

Mum complained that night that she could even smell mice at the table. It was little wonder. I had picked up many hundreds by the tail that afternoon. I felt sated, just like our cat.

Louey Marsh, the new schoolteacher, couldn't abide me; the feeling was mutual.

I handed her an envelope Mum had given me containing my birth certificate on the first day I returned to the school.

'What is your name?' she asked.

'Patricia Jean Smith,' I replied. 'I am usually called Jean.'

'Smith?' she said, 'Smith?' looking down at the birth certificate in her hand. I had never seen this, it was always sealed by Mum before she handed it to me.

'Smith?' she asked again.

A fear grabbed me and my heart shook. 'Smith is my name, isn't it?' I appealed to the kids, who of course remembered me.

'Yes,' they chorused. 'That's her name.'

I was still standing in front of the teacher's desk; she had not allotted me a place.

'So this is the clever little girl?' said this strange woman, attacking again. I was very frightened, but I stared straight back at her and said, 'Yes.'

She was extremely angry about that, and fear of her and rage at her battled within me. Goodness knows what she had been told about me.

I had never met a teacher like this one. At Caldermeade we'd had a man who would chase the boys up and down the aisles between the desks lashing at them with a strap of leather as they ran. This woman was coldly, surely insanely, cruel. Not for her the temper of heat.

I wrote a note on my slate later to Ted Jorgenson.

'Is she always mad?'

'Yes,' he wrote back. 'She takes a fit and hates a person. She hates anyone clever like Dorothy Fowler.'

In a matter of hours I saw clear evidence of this when she went directly to the frail child and hit her across chilblain-covered legs. This girl had the worst chilblains I ever saw, and I saw plenty because many children seemed to suffer with them in those days. Mostly they occurred on the hands only, but Dorothy had them on her legs, and her poor feet were so swollen with them that they wouldn't fit into shoes. To protect the broken sores her mother bound her feet into an old pair of felt slippers that had belonged to an adult.

When the teacher hit her Dorothy just stood and stared, petrified. Big tears rolled silently down her cheeks.

'Put out your hands,' the teacher said.

Instead of putting them out the girl lifted them dully in front of her eyes, the hands covered with fingerless mittens, the fingers sticking out of the ends like blue sausages, marbled, repulsive. Perhaps, as sometimes happens with bad chilblains, the pain was so intense that they were numb and dead.

'Put out your hands,' the woman said again. We were all watching, silent. Suddenly, quietly, Ted Jorgenson stood up.

'I'll take them,' he said.

It was the time-honoured rule that if an older child offered to take the cuts for a younger the offer must be accepted. Miss Marsh gave Ted ten of the best for his chivalry.

Children have great loyalty to a teacher; perhaps it is more to the dedicated profession they represent than the individual. We did not tell our parents about Louey Marsh, but we spoke about her calmly among ourselves without any of the rancour most teachers receive at some time in their career from thoughtless children. We knew this woman was sick. Mostly we supported one another against her, sometimes she made sure this would not be possible. She provided sweets for the whole school once to ensure their alienation from Kevin and me.

We two were the only Catholics at the school. This day a minister of religion came out from Numurkah to give instruction to the children. Because our parents had ordered us not to attend this class Louey Marsh sent Kevin to empty the two lavatory pans, and me to scrub the seats of the boys' and girls' lavatories. Before the other kids could rally to our defence she announced, 'A lolly scramble for the Bible class!' She knew that many of those children had sweets only at Christmas and would not be able to resist her bribe.

SUCH IS LIFE

I t was still the 1930s, a time when men were on top of the
world today and in the bankruptcy court tomorrow.

At Waaia when the effects of the Depression hit people
we were surprised. At Monomeith we saw the effects regularly
as men from the country jumped the rattler heading down to
the Big Smoke to look for work and men from the city headed
for the country, equally sure there must be work there for willing
hands. Waaia being on the track to nowhere, no one came
through looking for work. Men merely left the place. But the
Depression took its toll here as everywhere, and this affected
us all as every man was part of the whole life in this small,
isolated community.

Dalton Beswick, 'Mrs B's' son from the hotel, had taken on

wheat-buying in a small way. Coming home from school in the afternoon Kevin and I saw two strange men approach him as he lumped wheat on his stack.

'They're policemen,' Joe Sartori, a little Italian kid, told us. 'They've come for him. He's gonna get hung.'

Half expecting to see this very punishment carried out before our eyes, we hurried over. What we heard and saw was exciting to us because we so rarely saw a policeman.

'Come down from up there,' they called to Dalton high on the stack. 'We want to talk to you.'

'What do you want to talk about?' Dalton said, climbing higher.

'Wheat-stealing.'

Well!

'I don't know anything about it.' Dalton was higher still.

'It seems pretty suspicious if you skulk up there. If you don't know anything about it why don't you come down and talk to us instead of having to shout from up there? Half the town can hear you.' (Half the town had by now gathered near the stack, if the detectives only knew it.)

Dalton scrambled down. Kevin and I mistimed our appearance at the other side of the stack, for by the time we got round there Dalton was handcuffed to one of the detectives and was being bundled into the car.

'They're taking him to Numurkah to hang him,' said Joe Sartori. Gee!

Dalton's dilemma was this: in between the time of sending a 'parcel' of wheat down on the train one afternoon and its arrival at the market in the city the following day the price had dropped. It was now worth less than what he had paid the grower, the money being on the books only as yet. Dalton had no money behind him; he had bought a lot more wheat that he had not yet paid out for; mice had ruined much of his stack.

He tried the extreme method of extricating himself by stealing wheat to sell as his own. The first that Waaia knew of it was the appearance of the detectives at the railway station to ask

Mum for her carbon copies of way-bills and books showing to whom she had issued trucks on certain days. Their fingers quickly traced down the names on both and on both stopped opposite Dalton's name. The wheat, they told Mum, had been stolen from a paddock between midnight and 1 a.m. three nights ago.

Two days after his arrest Dalton arrived home on bail, his face blackened and bruised on one side, his lips cut.

'It certainly is an experience,' he told Dad. Dad brought him down to the house for a cup of tea.

'You don't want to let it get you down,' Dad said.

'Oh, no,' said Dalton. 'It's an experience, something different.'

He had brought a new piece of music out from Numurkah, 'Angeline'.

'Play it for me,' he asked. I played and he sang. 'Oh she was sweet sixteen, little Angeline.' Dalton was seventeen.

Mum was summonsed to appear at the court proceedings. She was to produce the station records concerning the truck that had transported the stolen wheat to Melbourne. All she had to do was to answer to her name and agree that these were the documents requested by the court, but Mum was so nervous that she was unable to work for days before and was just as ill for days after. She had never been inside a court before. She was so paralysed with nerves that she hardly noticed what was going on and could tell us little. This was disappointing because we had no conception of a court of law. The only thing of interest she could remember was that there were ten bags of wheat in the courtroom, some of it the stolen wheat, the rest brought from various farms. The farm-hand who had sewn the stolen bags was brought as witness and was to recognise the stolen bags by his sewing. When asked in the witness box if he could do this he replied, 'Among the sewing of a hundred men I would know mine. Any good bagger would.'

He did, and sewed two bags to demonstrate to the judge how he 'finished off with a double hitch sort of round the ear with a sort of loop if you see what I mean.' All the judge said as he watched the amazing speed of the man was, 'Goodness gracious!'

Dalton came home a free man. Though the tracks of his old truck were traced to the paddock it was held as the opinion of the court that the truck could have been used without Dalton's knowledge. Also it was the court's opinion that Dalton could not have moved the one hundred bags of wheat from the ground to the truck in the short period of time during which the theft had taken place. This became the joke of Waaia for some time: that a man could never brag about such a feat! (It was not considered at all impossible by many; Bill Martin could have lifted twice as many in that time and Dalton, well, nobody was willing to speak of what they knew of Dalton's strength and speed.)

Dalton didn't get into trouble again, and he didn't let this unpleasantness affect his life. He had courage, nerve, guts, faith – whatever you like to call it. Many had not.

One Saturday going into Numurkah on the Casey, Dad saw the car of a friend of ours near a bridge and slowed down, thinking to have a talk with the man. Then he saw our friend . . . and revved the motor up fast, hoping Mum had not seen what he had seen, and went on into the town to report to the police that Reg Dillon was lying dead beneath the bridge with a rifle barrel in what was left of his mouth.

That night at home, Dad said, 'If a man could only have a mate to talk to at these times. It's a mate you need for just those few moments when there seems to be no other way out. But such is life.'

The next blow fell very close. Kevin Young's family went bankrupt. 'Just like that,' the grown-ups repeated over and over again. We children couldn't understand. We stared in disbelief at their colonial-style home and solid British-made furniture that Mum had told us was now seized and would be sold. We wandered through their garden with its trellises weighed down by vines under which we would lie and eat grapes in the cool of the night while our parents sat in canvas chairs relaxing after the heat of the day. There were the chicken hatcheries and the poultry pens that housed thousands of laying hens – sidelines to wheat-buying – where we'd watched chickens hatch and gathered eggs with the workmen, and the gristing mill where each morning Kevin's father would process the newly garnered wheat into meal for the morning's porridge.

All this was to go under the hammer. Kevin and I walked disconsolately round the places we loved. The front of the house had been a shop before the wheat-buying became big business, and the size and wealth of that new business were evident in the stock still left in the store which there had been no need to realise on when the golden grain brought such a fortune. Kevin and I played shop there and sold to one another rolls and reels of ribbons and laces and broderie anglaise, cottons, needles and tins of goods. There were scales for weighing things, counters with rulers let into them to measure materials, a till that 'pinged' when we put our cardboard money in it. Now this would all go.

We went over to the workman's cottage, empty beside the bamboo plantation; we had used this as a make-believe home whenever it was unoccupied, and we wished now to take away and keep a picture we had used to decorate the wall. Kevin held the picture in his hands and as we walked out the cottage door big 'Bull' Marvel grabbed him by the arm.

'Don't try that,' he snarled. 'Trying to sneak things.' He swore at Kevin and called him a dirty name and said his father was no longer the 'big boss cocky'. It was the only time I ever heard anyone speak poorly to that boy. I cried and went home. Dad told me we must forgive 'Bull' his hate because he had never had love, family, a proper home or money to spend.

'These are strange times to be living through,' he said. 'All we can hope to do is lend a hand when someone needs it.' Dad wasn't to know how soon he would need a hand himself and how readily help would be forthcoming because of the many times his own tough, callused hand had stretched out towards others. But this was later.

Kevin at times would be grave with concern for his parents – he could see that they were distressed – but at other times he would be a young boy and forget. One such time was when his mother scolded him.

'I shan't stop with you,' he said. 'I'll go where my friends are.' He packed a bag with pyjamas, a packet of biscuits and his old teddy-bear which he hadn't taken to bed for many a year, and came to us. Mum sent Mickie across to tell Mrs Young he was safe and would bed down at our house. But when it grew dark he began to fidget and then he said, 'I think I'd better have a look and see if Mum and Dad are all right.' And off he went with his bag on his back.

The family were allowed to keep only those things necessary to continue to exist – a bed each and little more. All else must be sold.

'How are things going?' Mrs Young asked Kevin and me when we came inside during the sale, which was held in the grounds.

With the thoughtlessness of children we said, 'Wonderful. They're selling things for almost nothing.' We had seen a cedar cabinet go for five shillings, a chest of drawers the family had brought out from England via India for ten shillings.

'It doesn't matter,' she said. 'Nothing matters.'

They went to Melbourne to look for work. The father, used to employing many men, now took a job as a carpenter's mate and shortly after fell from high scaffolding and broke his neck. Mrs Young, a skilled dressmaker who had done her apprenticeship to the trade in Europe, opened a high-class salon in the city and soon was dressing many of Melbourne's socialites. One night, visiting a friend in hospital, she was knocked over by a car driven by an unlicensed youth and was partly crippled. At that time an outbreak of 'infantile paralysis' was ravaging Australian cities, so Kevin was left to live with us at Waaia until that should ease.

GETTING OUR IRISH UP

I was twelve when I won my first race. Mick had, of course, left school. Jack, who had come from the orphanage to live with us, was working as a bricklayer's labourer; he carried a hod of bricks up a ladder all day and was so enthusiastic that he brought the hod home to demonstrate to us at night. I was doing the Merit Certificate at school.

I still sat between Ted Jorgenson and Alan Thornton, but we had a new teacher. He was a type unknown to us and we distrusted him at first; he didn't hit girls! And he encouraged us to read – even to read newspapers – and to enter sports contests with other schools. He bought us a radio with Mothers' Club money so that we could listen to the Schools Broadcasts, which were then only beginning.

Soon I idolised him. He opened up for me a new world of learning – *and* under his guidance I won my first race. I was at Numurkah at the district school sports. Waaia girls went into 'uniform' for the day, white cotton dresses the mothers had cut out in the hall on the long trestle supper tables, and gold head-bands. We were a fine-looking lot by the time we were eventually bumped into the big town on the tray of Dalton Beswick's wheat truck. I was proud even to be competing, but to win! Mum saw my triumph, but I had to wait till we returned home to tell Dad.

'Which race?' he asked, almost as excited as I was.

'The egg and spoon.'

Oh, the pride of me to see him begin to smile and then to laugh!

'You little bobby-dazzler,' he said. 'You're a little hum-dinger.' He pinned the blue ribbon on my dress. For night on night he had tried to train me along the side of the railway track with no success. Now he asked me to come out and demonstrate my winning style. Mum and Dad and Mick and Kevin and Jack all came to watch. Mick, who could fly like a silver streak, competed against me, and so did Kevin, but I beat them easily. They walked, or ran slowly, crouched over, afraid the egg would drop if they wobbled the spoon. Holding the spoon in the way Mr Schmidt the teacher had shown me, I ran at the same speed I always did and won. Dad came over.

'Give me a look in your mouth,' he said. I carefully levered the handle of the spoon out and he looked in. I had had two teeth out and the gaps held the spoon so firmly it couldn't budge.

This race gave Dad ideas for further contests that I might be successful in. For instance, Mick could ride a bike faster than me – most kids with two legs could.

'Why not a slow bicycle race?' Dad suggested. He made up the rules; no turning back, no putting the feet to the ground, etc. Kevin and I practised every morning and every night until in the end when we challenged the whole school we two beat them easily. We could hold our bikes almost at a standstill indefinitely by moving the handle-bars a fraction, so twisting the front wheels as a balance. We were still near the starting line when the others had crossed the finish.

Ted and Alan still gave me larry-dooley. I was twelve and they were fourteen years old and we were all going to sit for the Merit exam. Their size and weight made me defer to them, my size and weight led them to bully me, but when the day came for us to go to another little bush school to do the exam we were all equal in our nervousness. Alan Thornton drove the three of us in the shay-cart his family came to school in, and we put our lunch bags under the flap, jogged off and hardly said a word the whole way.

Three weeks later the results came back. We had all passed. Ted and Alan would leave school and go to work. I wanted to learn much more.

'What is there to learn now?' said the boys. 'We've got our Merit.'

I had sat for three scholarships and was awarded all three. 'Until my dying day,' Mum said as I stamped out, laughing hard, shouting, 'I don't care! I didn't want them anyway!' because I never let anyone know when I was hurt beyond speech, 'Till my dying day I will never forgive them. The advertisements were lies, all of them. "Free scholarships!" Now she's won them they tell us they aren't free! She can't go, and they lied.'

It was no use Mr Schmidt telling her that no, the colleges had not lied, but they were totally unaware of the financial straits of a family living on the 'emergency reduction of wages' that had been dropped on wage earners like a threatening hand on 12 February that year.

'Free?' she said. 'And here on the letters they list the costs of uniforms and all the other things.'

'The scholarships are for tuition only,' Mr Schmidt explained.

'But how can a country girl whose father earns £2 19s 4d a week, whose mother gets nothing except the house rent-free for running the station for twelve hours a day six days a week, how can she get uniforms and travel and "the extras" they

mention . . . and there's only one of them offers her a bed!'
Mum had been loud, but now she became still and silent, staring
at the papers spread on the kitchen table; then she spoke so
quietly I could hardly hear her. 'She won't be able to go and
she's tried and tried. How can they . . . the thing is, they don't
know how people are hanging on out here in the bush. They
don't know about us.'

Out at the stunted-for-water nectarine tree I heard the terrible
noise begin, the deep sobbing that would humiliate her to have
been caught in front of anyone at all. The teacher came out.
'You should go to your mother.' He put his arm around my
shoulder and it felt like a log. 'Her hurt is as bad as yours.'

Mum stopped crying when I came in and turned on me in
frustration. All the hard years, the pride in never letting on that
they were hard years, boiled over. 'You and your Little Miss-
Muck scholarships!'

I took the papers from the kitchen table, tore them up and
threw the pieces in the wood-fire stove. 'I didn't want to go
to their flash schools anyhow!'

This new teacher had made my mind sit up and look around
for the first time. Perhaps I might even . . . I whispered and
the teacher had to bend to hear . . . perhaps even the university . . . then I became embarrassed and pretended that I hadn't
meant it and was fooling; I hadn't heard those words spoken
in any school I had attended; I hadn't known what one could
do in a university until this teacher told me of the open, unfenced
plain of learning one could embark on there. But to blurt out
that I of all people wanted to go – they'd all laugh at me for
sure . . .

'University!' said Mr Schmidt. 'University?' He looked
unseeing at me, thinking.

Then, 'Yes, why not! Why not? You can do it. You do it
and take all of us along with you, because you'll do correspondence lessons here at the school.'

When the first lessons arrived everyone in the school crowded
round to have a look. The first papers to be taken out of the

package were the French lessons. That fixed it. I was a scholar.

Mr Schmidt looked up the programme to see when the French lessons were broadcast. I sat staring at the radio. The voice was speaking slowly, loudly, but I had no idea what it was saying. The other kids giggled at the alien sound of the voice, but naturally I didn't, I was a scholar! And I was learning French! The truth of the matter is that as time went by I learnt to read and write the language a little, but to this day I can neither 'hear' nor speak it, this being the fault, I believe, of learning by eye and not at all by ear.

Learning at an advanced stage by correspondence is not easy. The teacher helped me when he could, but his first consideration must be to his eight school curriculum grades, and sometimes weeks would pass and he'd not be able to spare time for me. The great benefit of doing the lessons in a schoolroom was the time-table and the enforced silence which one could not get in one's own home. A drawback to the whole scheme was the mailing of work for corrections. This week's work might not be returned until the week after next, by which time I'd be busy with a different problem and would have no interest in the work I'd done so long ago, not even to look at the corrections.

Because of the drawbacks of this system of learning I was told that an extra year of study would be added onto my time before I could take the Leaving for matriculation. Correspondence education is not the best means of gaining knowledge, but when there is nothing else it is the very best.

At home there was a quickening too: the courting of Kathleen-cum-Mick had begun. From being all gangly legs and uncontrolled arms and ungainly body she had become quite beautiful with a perfect figure. Even the long, tight, cotton 'bodies' that Mum encased us in could not conceal Mick's curves. The boys of the town were quick to notice this.

At the next Waaia Race Ball she wore her first evening gown, red velvet, plain with a square neckline. I couldn't take my eyes from her, neither could half the men in the hall. Towards the end of the evening the son of our local MP approached Mum and said, 'Mrs Smith, will you give me permission to walk Kathleen home?'

Mum tried to rise to the occasion, but all she eventually thought of was, 'You'll have to ask her father.'

Dad naturally said, 'Oh, I wouldn't know about that. It's up to her mother.' The poor boy shuttled backwards and forwards between the pair of them. Eventually Mum agreed.

No doubt the boy didn't know it, but this permission meant merely that he could walk home with the bunch of us in the midst of whom was Kathleen-cum-Mick. I, the young sister, could not have been any inducement to romance either because I glued myself to the young couple in case I missed anything. This was my first experience of courting. I need not have been so anxious.

The courting of Kathleen was on with a vengeance from that night onwards. Knowing of the hospitality of Mum and Dad, young bloods would stroll along ostensibly for a 'yarn' or a game of tennis. Some Sunday nights there were three suitors sitting side by side at the tea table or singing together round the piano.

Not that Mick did much to encourage them. She had no pretensions. We could all get our Irish up in this household – all except sanguine Dad, that is – but when Mick cut loose she was a tornado. More dangerous even than her temper was her ability to rouse others.

'She'll die with her boots on,' was Dad's comment the day her brother Jack tried to hit her with a log of wood. It was Saturday. Jack was building me a shelter in which to keep my private things down the yard, using four red-gum sleepers for the corner posts. I coaxed him to come looking for mushrooms across the paddocks and while he was gone Mick cut through the sleepers. We heard the axe as we were coming home.

'That's my sleeper,' Jack shouted immediately. He knew Mickie.

By the time I reached home they had nearly exhausted themselves. Mick had seen him coming and had dropped the axe and run. He picked up the end of the sleeper and ran after her. Had he caught her he could have brained her with one blow of that mighty weapon, but our Mick was fleet. I walked past them into the house. I didn't know what else to do. This apparent disregard steadied them, and soon Mick ran inside too and Jack satisfied himself by threatening her from the door: 'If you so much as show your face!'

The son of the MP arrived in full courting rig one night to find Jack hitting Mick's head intently on the kitchen floor. She had taken his kerosene tin of bath water off the top of the stove and tipped it out.

I was often driven quite strongly mad by her teasing. Mum and Dad were away on the Casey on a Saturday inspection trip and we were supposed to have the breakfast dishes done by their return.

'You do the dishes, I want to read,' Mick ordered me, hauling out her *Peg's Paper* from its hiding place under the cushion on Mum's chair.

'I want to read,' I complained. I had *The Wind in the Willows*.

'You wash up or I'll get rid of these.' They were the gifts I'd prepared for Mum's birthday the following day, a card I'd painted and a handkerchief sachet made from a piece of material from the scrap bag.

I knew she meant what she said but I tried to bluff it out. I picked up my book. Mick leant over and carefully pushed the card under the hot soapy water in the wash-up dish, and as it disappeared the water coloured with paints as they ran. I hit out at her and as I watched it her little finger split in two its entire length and lay open. I still held the carving knife I had been washing when Mum left.

We were both so surprised we did nothing for a bit, then I got bandages and bound the two pieces tightly together. I cuddled her and she was laughing and I was crying. When Mum returned we told her Mick had 'nicked' it on a knife as she washed up, so it wasn't examined until the following day and by then it had begun to heal so well that it was left as it was and Mick to this day has a little finger with a ridge.

Mum used to say that she couldn't understand these rages against Mick . . . until the day Mick came in rubbing a lump on her head, and a bewildered Mum holding the tin dipper in her hand followed her.

'I don't know what made me do it,' Mum said over and over again. 'I don't know what came over me.'

The rest of the household knew just how she felt, except Dad, but then he was never put out by anything.

Some of Mick's suitors were a little more than bewildered by our goings on, but no concessions were made, they would see us as we were and Mick, too, because none of us knew how to be any different.

Mick led all her suitors a merry dance. She teased them all as mercilessly as she had us until the boy I shall call Bob came along.

Bob had been forced to leave high school when his parents could no longer afford to keep him there. He had worked his way from Numurkah up the shearing route to Queensland and by his twentieth birthday had worked his way back again.

Dad was holding gymnasium practice for footballers in the big wheat shed, bringing to bear the training he had received during World War I in the Royal Australian Navy. Mum provided supper for the men, cooking two to three dozen meat pies and a kerosene tin full of coffee for them. One night Bob came down to help carry the coffee.

'This is my daughter,' Mum introduced Mick. Bob looked at her, beautiful, flushed from the heat of the cooking, her red-gold hair tied in a ribbon. She ignored him.

'Yes,' said Bob. 'A real country girl.'

Kathleen-cum-Mick had met her match.

20

DAD! DAD!

This year summer came in with a blast like an open oven door. Swaggies limped by, sweat staining the backs of their shirts where the swag rubbed. Often before they came up to the house seeking hot water for their billies they would rest for a time under the shade of the big gum in our horse paddock where Sylvia and I had met the day we played swaggies. One said to my mother as she boiled water for his billy, 'You can trace my footsteps from here to Cunnamulla, missus. There's not been a breath of wind nor a drop of rain for twelve months to wipe them out.' Birds came in wearily to rest in the drooping greenery of our pepper-corn trees. On Sundays when we must study our catechisms we would sit under those trees and the birds would nosey down to see what we were doing. Now they perched listlessly, their chattering only half the volume it was in the days of rain showers. The only breeze we got was an occasional willy-willy that swirled the red dust round covering everything and creeping in everywhere. That Christmas a small freak shower came out of the blue cloudless sky and disappeared within minutes leaving the sky blue and cloudless as before, and the only thing to prove to us that it had rained was Bob's red shirt. He had been out walking with Mick when the shower surprised them and he had put his jacket over her head and they ran for home, he in his white shirt. By the time they got in the door his shirt was red as rust. We had seen this phenomenon before and called it 'red rain'; it was caused by moisture falling through the thick blanket of red dust that was perpetually above our land.

January continued hot. The stillness and heat were sombre. The rail men made inspection runs back along the line after each steam train passed to ensure that no errant spark could start a fire. The wheat was golden and tinder-dry. The grass on the side of the line was the same. The men were trying to burn it off, working mostly at night.

For four days in succession the thermometer read 105 in the shade. On that fourth day Dad lay on the track with his broken face resting on the rail that now seared flesh, his poor shattered body exposed to this killing heat. Five hours passed before his unconscious body was found.

He had been home late before, but this night he wasn't ten minutes overdue when Mum began to fidget. 'Go and see if your father's trike's in the shed,' she said to me. No, there was no sign of him. 'You might just look up the line and see if he's coming.' But he wasn't coming. In a while, 'Go and put your ear to the rail. See if you can hear anything.' There was no sound or vibration in that blistering, mirage-washed heat. 'He isn't coming,' I reported.

Mum set our tea for us and left to walk a few miles of the track in case he had broken down. It was too late to phone Nathalia or Picola railway stations, in the direction from which he should be travelling home. The stations would be closed and the phones could not be heard from the houses. It was 8 p.m. when Mum came back, alone. We sensed the despair in her. 'It's nearly dark. He should be home.' She sent us girls to the hotel to tell them there that Dad wasn't home. 'Then he's in trouble,' Dalton Beswick said. 'I'll get the truck cranked up. Get your mother and we'll look for him.'

His truck, the one on which the stolen wheat had supposedly been transported, was a 1924 model and Mick and I stood on the tray at the back, hanging onto the top of the cabin while Mum sat in front with Dalton. The road ran level with the rail track and he steered the truck with one hand and beamed a flashlight across on the rails with the other. Six miles further on the headlights of a car approached us. 'That's them,' said Mum. 'Who?' 'They've found him,' she replied with certainty. 'Pull up.' She walked across to the other car as it came abreast of us, and the driver guessed who she would be. 'Hop in, Mrs Smith,' he said. Then he got out and came across to Dalton. 'Take her kids home,' he said. 'He won't go for an hour or so yet, so she mightn't be home till morning.'

'As bad as that?' Dalton asked.

'They're putting the pieces of his trike into sugar-bags.'

Dalton knew we heard. He sat us in the front of the truck with him. He did things on the way home in an attempt to make us forget what we had heard. He sang, whistled, drove fast, drove slow, silly things to keep our numbed thoughts from that solid iron and hardwood motor-trike that was now fragmented and bundled into sugar-bags. At the hotel he put us to bed and made lumpy cocoa. 'You don't want to worry,' he said. 'You don't want to worry.' But he was only seventeen and he was crying too, so he put the lamp out and left us.

All the next day Mick and I had no word. I had never communicated easily, neither had she. Now we couldn't ask if he were still alive and no one thought to tell us. I prayed and Mick prayed and when we finished our gentle pleading entreaties I continued savagely in silence: 'If You kill him I'll kill You.'

21

DAD . . .

He was still alive four days later. They said he must die this night. Mick and I were taken to see him late in the hot silent afternoon. Nathalia had opened a Bush Nursing Hospital to take him in and provided a nursing sister. There, in the dimness of the blind-drawn room, he lay on the tarpaulin on which he'd been carried from the track. The wise bush nurse knew that to move him further would be to precipitate the death that was merely biding its time. Some of his clothes she had cut from him, others had become embedded in his torn flesh, cemented there by dried blood. He was black from the blood and sunburn. Our mother was sitting beside his bed: in that way we recognised him. One eye was closed, the other had disappeared and the gaping socket showed. There was a clean white sheet over him, but thick woollen blankets above that to counter the shivers of shock. I stared, trying to see the father who had called me Jeanie-weanie-cat's-eyes and Paddy-the-next-best-thing. As I looked he moaned like an animal with his mouth only half open and rolled his blackened head. I cried out and ran from the room. Mick had kissed him. I wished I had.

Old Nip was sitting on the verandah of the hospital. He had been with Dad at the time of the accident. When the men found Dad, Nip was standing guard keeping the crows from him, snapping and leaping at them as they came for flesh. One side of Dad's face was lying on the rail, but the other side was exposed and this was clear of dirt and ants where Nip had been licking him in distress. The old dog had never bitten anyone in his life. Now he turned into a mad thing and like a wolf tried to savage the men when they lifted Dad onto the tarpaulin. It was impossible to remove the body with the dog raving as he was. One of the gang had to knock him out with a piece of the shattered trike and he was carried into Nathalia beside Dad. They took him to Waaia, but he found his way back to the hospital and sat whining outside and scratching on the door. He refused to eat. The fettlers tried to coax him away, but he wouldn't budge. He was howling badly at night and the nursing sister was afraid that it distressed Mum as she sat waiting. This afternoon as we watched, the ganger came and threw a bag over him and carried him away as gently as if he were a child.

'I'll look after him for your Dad,' he told us.

Then the Catholic church bell began to ring. It was calling people to prayers for Dad as it did each evening. There was something terribly heart-hurting to hear that tinny little bell tinkling for Dad.

As we waited to be taken back to Waaia the fettlers trooped up as they did daily to ask after him and bring a piece of ice. Ice was normally carried during the hot months by the 'Beetle' in the top of the canvas water bag strapped to the outside of the ugly little train. Now all that was left of it when they got to Nathalia was quickly wrapped in wet hessian by the guard and handed to the fettlers, who ran it up to the hospital.

When his swollen tongue recovered he began to speak, rambling in the delirium of unconsciousness.

'Creek water,' he begged, and Mum rubbed pieces of the ice around his black lips and trickled iced milk down his throat. A bed had been moved to his room for Mum.

One night he became wild and began to move in the bed. Mum, afraid he would harm his broken body, called the sister to come. The doctor came too. By then he was speaking, rambling they thought at first, but then as they understood what he was saying they stared in amazement. The doctor and nurse sat beside Mum on her bed and listened to him.

Amid the thunder in his head he could hear the guns of Jutland as the great naval battle began. Then the noise abated and he was a young boy again going to sea for the first time, lonely, afraid. As the listeners stared at him he sailed through the oceans of the world, anchored off Rabaul and went ashore when war was declared, captured the German radio station and took prisoner-of-war all the personnel.

'The captain said when we came back on board that we weren't Jack-tars. He said we were Jacks-of-all-trades,' he laughed, reliving his youth as he lay there blinded, done for.

'There was one of our submarines came into Rabaul. We had only two – the *AE1* and the *AE2*. I wanted to go on the *AE1*. My mate went on it. I got a fever and was put in our sick bay.' His voice faltered. 'Goodbye, *AE1*,' he said, and great tears welled from his eye that hadn't been lubricated for weeks.

'Poor Jack. The winding sheet of steel.' *AE1* had sailed from the harbour and was never heard of again.

'I wrote a poem about *AE1*,' he said. (Mum found it later, carefully hidden among his private papers.)

Then he sailed to the Panama Canal. 'They were neutral. They wouldn't let us through. We headed south. We went through the Straits of Magellan. There wasn't much room. The charts weren't much good. No ship as big as us had been there before.

It was dark beneath the cliffs. That's where Magellan's men became afraid.'

The three listeners heard of the war at sea, heard of his ship being out of sight of land for eighteen months, refuelling and revictualling at sea.

'I had my seventeenth birthday and my eighteenth and didn't see land in between,' the broken man on the bed said.

Then, 'I was in hospital for a long time in London. When I began to walk round a Lord Someone asked would three Australian sailors like to be his guests for the evening. I went and two others. He took us to dinner first. I hadn't tasted strong drink before and that night we had champagne. Then we went up into a balcony box in the theatre. His wife was with us but she was old. We leant over the edge of the box and saw some young girls sitting down below. One smiled at me so I climbed over the side and slid down a pillar and sat on her knee.'

Later he fell in love with a famous singer and she with him.

'I've got things she gave me at home,' he said. (We found these too. Among them was a wallet with a notebook in which she had written the words of the song she had helped to make famous: 'Dearest, the day is over, ended the dream divine, you must go back to your life, I must go back to mine.' In a pocket of the wallet was a note from her begging to be allowed to join him in Australia.)

It amused us in later years to hear Mum describe this night. She spoke of Dad's description of sea battles and experiences as 'accurate to the last detail', but dismissed his escapades on shore as 'ramblings'.

Five weeks after he was carried in Dad opened his one remaining eye and said, 'Hello, Birdie. How long have I been here?' For answer she laid her head beside his and thanked God over and over again.

All the while he had been unconscious little had been done to mend his broken body. At first they waited for him to die. Then it was all they could do to keep him alive. Now the

142

Railways Department at their own expense sent up a Melbourne specialist. This man examined him and thought it might be worth an attempt to get him to Melbourne for a series of operations.

'But I can promise nothing, Mrs Smith. If he lives he may be insane. He has received more than the limit of injuries the human body can take. By all medical law he should not be alive.'

We never found the cause of the accident. All we knew was that he had been coming home early in the afternoon to have a rest before going back in the cool of the evening to burn off dry grass. He had only travelled five miles from the gang. The fettlers believed that an elderly woman who lived beside the track had put her cows on the line to graze and that Dad had hit one. They examined the cows, but none were marked. There was no sign of any other living thing on the line.

Dad admitted to a liking for speed. He once set his inspection motor in a race against Fred Jorgenson's T Model Ford for nine miles and beat him home. But had the accident been caused by speed then, by the fettlers' reckoning and the later inquiry, the trike would not have been much damaged. It would merely have jumped the line. His trike was shattered to small pieces, and he was shattered too, yet his dog was unmarked. It has remained a mystery.

As soon as Dad could be moved a guard's van was shunted into the siding; the fettlers carried him in on a stretcher, secured it firmly and set up a chair for Mum. These big, strong, brown men looked down at the ravaged face and said, 'You'll be right as rain, Albert. They'll have you back in no time.' 'It's an old dog for a hard road, you know.'

The engine-driver looked in and said, 'We'll take it easy, mate, you'll be right.' Then the steam whistle blew on the engine and the train began to jolt slowly forward. There is a corny, melodramatic old song that reminds me of that journey. It begins, 'As the train rolled onwards, a mother sat in tears, dreaming of the happiness of all the bygone years . . .' Disc jockeys ride it with their wisecracks today, but it can send my thoughts to love, gentleness, hope and trust as quickly as can Bach's 'Sheep May Safely Graze'. The pioneers of the American backwoods had troubles, hopes and fears like those of the pioneers of the Australian bush, and this accounts to a great degree for the adoption by us of much of their folk music.

Dad stayed in hospital in Melbourne for six months and came home walking, sane and with two sighted eyes. His absent eye was discovered undamaged beneath his cheek bone. To us he looked wonderful. Like the lovers in the enchanted cottage who could not see one another's defects we were so happy to be together again that we didn't notice any change in his looks.

22

KINDNESS AND COURAGE

There was change we did notice. Dad couldn't work. The Railways Department allowed Mum to stay on as station-mistress. Her wage was fifteen shillings a week with the house rent-free. She tried to keep out of debt. The piano was still being paid off.

'Let it go,' the relatives urged her. 'Why put yourself in debt for *her*?' That was me.

'We'll manage,' Mum said.

She received plenty of advice, but not much of the only help that was any good at the time – £ s d.

There was an auction sale at Marvels' place one day and she sent me over with some things she packed up. We were desperately in need of money then. Dad needed to have food that cost much; there was no cheap way to feed such a sick man. Mum thought she would get about thirty shillings for the box of goods at the sale. When I returned to the auctioneer that night he handed me 1s 9d. The walk home to Mum was long.

It seemed ironical that those who gave practical help never gave a word of advice along with it.

That Christmas, though things were thin, Mum never let us know about it. The puddings were cooked and threepences and sixpences put in them, poultry was killed and cooked and enough cakes were baked to fill a cream can. The bath was the storage place for two dozen bottles of home-made ginger beer, and the Coolgardie safe had jellies and custards setting within. Mrs Beswick from the hotel regularly brought tempting dishes for Dad, most of which he was unable to eat, so we had these stored away too. The strangest gifts came from the most unexpected people.

A few days before Christmas an old Indian hawker who used to camp in our paddock arrived.

'Your man still bad?' he asked Mum. She nodded to the distance, where Dad wandered painfully alone.

'You give me five bob for a good cardigan to keep him warm,' he said, unable to resist making some sort of sale but ready to lose heavily on the deal. It was a beautiful cardigan, thick and warm and worth twenty-five shillings in the shops.

The Chinese market gardener with the old horse nodding in front of his cart came the same as usual.

'Melly Clissmus, missus,' he beamed, handing Mum the traditional jar of ginger in syrup. Then he turned to us girls. 'Melly Clissmus, missee,' he wished each of us, and pushed a large parcel into our arms.

'Hopee Mister Smith better soon. Tell him melly Clissmus too.' And smiling from ear to ear he drove off.

'But I want vegetables,' Mum called.

'Melly Clissmus,' he carolled back, his round, yellow face poked out the side of the moving wagon.

Our vegetables were in the parcel he had given Mick, and there was fruit in the parcel I held. There was everything we could have wished for: lettuces, new carrots, new potatoes, spring onions, parsley, mint, green peas, marrow, asparagus and tomatoes, apples, bananas and a big red watermelon.

'Holy Father in heaven bless that little yellow man,' Mum prayed that night, and we all said, 'Amen', and Dad who didn't pray said, 'Too right!'

For some time now we had had no visits from the swagmen. They gave our place a wide berth. On Christmas Eve a man went by just before sundown, heading for the wheat shed, his back bowed in the heat beneath his bluey. Dad saw him and went in to confer with Mum.

'Take this to him and tell him to have a Christmas drink to wash the dust down,' Dad said to me and sent me off. I went up the line after the swaggie and called out. I told him what Dad had said. He flipped the two shilling piece in the air reflectively.

'It wouldn't be half bad,' he said. Then, 'How is your dad, girlie? Any better?' I told him yes, that he might be able to work soon.

'Then I'll have a drink and like it all the better because it came from Albert Smith,' he said. I nearly burst with pride. As I scampered off home he called, 'And tell your Mum God bless her too.' I'd never heard such talk outside my own home!

'Well,' said Dad when I told him the swagmen knew he had been ill. 'Can you beat that? Word must have gone up the track.'

23

THE
CONVENTUAL
LIFE

I had not been confirmed in the Church and as I was twelve
years old the time was ripe for this 'giving of the Holy
Ghost'. This ceremony was so important and we were so
far from religious instruction that it was decided I should be
cared for at the convent in Numurkah and attend classes there.
This came to be one of the happiest periods of my life.

The convent at Numurkah was not a boarding school but
merely a large house wherein lived the nuns who taught at the
day school there. I had a wonderful time with them and I think
they had the same with me.

Mum and Mickie drove off home and left me alone in the
little bare room that was to be mine until the day of
confirmation. A narrow bed, single, the first I had ever slept

in, a wardrobe of my own, a window of ripple glass and a bare board floor. As I stood contemplating the isolation, the wonder and terror of having a room of my own, there came a knock on my door. No one had ever knocked on my door before. An elderly nun came in.

'We thought perhaps you'd like to be alone to unpack,' she said, a little nervously perhaps. I wondered if they were as unsure of me as I was of them. What to do with a little girl in their spare bedroom was exercising their thoughts already.

'You don't want to unpack?'

'Not much.' I didn't know what to do with unpacking. On our annual holiday trips we always left our clothes in our suitcases. Besides, Mum was diffident about the clothes I had. She had knitted me a dress of heavy silk, there was another dress she had made me from a wine-coloured coat she had been given, and a cotton dress. I had black stockings, the black boots that I wore to strengthen my ankles and which were still 'wearing out', two nightdresses (one new), two pairs of fleecy-lined pants, and singlets. And of course a hat with a big brim to keep the sun off my face. I had never been without a hat in my life.

The nuns were filing down the corridor to their chapel for prayers.

'Take a book out into the sun,' the Mother Superior said. 'Roll your stockings down. Have a sun-bake.' I could scarcely believe my ears. Read? Sun-bake? I thought it would be prayers non-stop. I'd never lain in the sun. My Irish colouring that Mum was so proud of would be ruined. I dragged a chair to the middle of the lawn, forgot to wear my broad-brimmed hat, rolled my stockings down, reached out and took the book nearest in the pile the nuns had left out for me, and abandoned myself.

Two weeks later when my mother came to fit me with the white silk dress she was making for the ceremony she took one look at me and shrieked.

'You look like an Indian!'

She was furious. 'How can you wear white with a face as black as that!' I had resurrected the black stockings when I knew she was coming, so she was spared the sight of my 'black' legs. And as she couldn't see inside me she didn't know that I was as 'black' inside as out. I had eaten, devoured, chewed up, swallowed and digested three books: *Daddy Long Legs*, *These Old Shades* and *Myself When Young*. And more was in store; the nuns had borrowed a whole stock of books for me from their students. Far from having to hide books, here they were thrust on me. I read every spare minute and I had plenty.

'A most intelligent little girl,' the nuns told the priest when he called to see how I was getting along. 'Reads all day.' Rarely can starvation have been mistaken for intelligence as it was here.

The ordered days were a delight. At 6 a.m. a nun would come into my room and touch my cheek, begin a prayer and leave the room when my sleepy voice took over from her. The nuns filed down the corridor to their chapel for prayers, smiling at me as they passed. Out in a vestibule on a tray a glass of warm milk awaited me before a radiator, my book lay on the table ready for me to read until breakfast was served.

I had long curls still and there was much fussing about them. I was too busy with my reading to take much notice, but one day I took a look in the hand mirror in the bathroom and was surprised at the smart hair-do I'd been given. This hand mirror surprised me too. Like most people outside a convent I had the dimmest ideas of conventual life. Certainly the nuns didn't primp and just as certainly they were the neatest women alive and needed a mirror occasionally to see to this neatness. They used sweet-scented toilet soap, and talc powder, and one nun there who taught piano used a skin perfume that was delicious as you sat beside her playing. They were ultra-feminine or, more exactly, completely feminine: all the masculinity a woman is born with had been dissolved. Their every movement, gesture and word was womanly, graceful, gentle, not only in the impression gained by the eye and ear but in the aura that surrounded them.

Yet they weren't precious. One night I heard a loud squealing noise. I leapt out of bed. Another scream. I ran out in my nightie.

There on the enclosed verandah four nuns were playing table tennis with an outfit they had been given that day. They played with gusto; one was very good and had played before, the rest were having a great time in a hit and giggle sort of way. Another time one was playing tennis with me. I ran up, pretending to jump the net and ducked under it at the last minute. She ran up, hitched up her skirt and sailed clear over the top.

In the daytime they wore the habit one usually sees them in. For bed they wore a long white shift and a white cap frilled all round the edge. The young ones looked nice in this. The older women looked like little gnomes with wisps of grey hair fluttering out from under their caps. I'd thought their heads were shaven and was very surprised to find some of them had quite long hair. I blundered into the bathroom one Saturday and found one nun cutting another's hair that was down past her ears and as black as mine in colour. She just hacked away happily until it was shorter and said, 'How's that?' The other sister felt it with her hands and said, 'That feels fine, thank you, sister,' and replaced the several layers of cloth on which to pin the outer veil.

Their life was ordered from getting up in the morning to going to bed at night. There was no fear of insecurity of body or soul for them. No lonely old age ahead or the worry of finding and keeping employment. Most of all, they knew where they were going just as surely as most of us do not know. I loved them then, I envy them now.

At last confirmation day was upon me. The night before I'd had a bath, washed my hair and gone into the chapel to pray and had put on the light and startled out of their wits the six nuns who were praying there in the dark. Hot with embarrassment I knelt there, not knowing whether to turn off the light or leave it on. Old Mother Superior solved that by coming to me and putting her arm round my shoulders.

'You'll get your death of cold in here after a hot bath,' she said. 'Come and I'll tuck you into your bed.'

'But I haven't said my rosary.'

'Say it in bed then.'

Mum would never believe me if I told her that!

Dad was to be confirmed this day too. Since his recovery he had learnt of the prayer and help of Catholics towards his recovery. He knew Mum prayed for his conversion. So this day Archbishop Mannix was to tap both of us on the cheek to remind us of the blows we must take for Christ and the strength we would need to follow Him.

How Mum must have scraped and done without herself to do this for me . . . a white silk dress, white stockings and black patent leather shoes with big silver buckles, white tulle veil and coronet of flowers. When the sponsor stood behind me, her hand on my shoulder, I was asked the name of the patron saint I had chosen. Because I'd been away from home no one had remembered to prepare me for this.

'Bridget,' I said, without hesitation, my mother's real name. Dad chose James, the name of his father, James Adam Smith.

To save him from appearing with us children, Dad was confirmed when the congregation had left the church. The Archbishop, who even then in the 1930s was known as 'old' Archbishop Mannix, came out of the sacristy and down to the altar rails. I knelt beside Dad. His face had healed well but the scars were fiery and the eye that had been thought lost was wild. He shook badly and held onto the wooden rail. His hand was near mine and our little fingers touched. I loved him very much. The Archbishop offered his hand first to Dad and then to me to kiss the great ring which was his seal of authority, blessed us and left us kneeling there together.

24

LAUGHTER
AND TEARS

Mick was to be married. It surprised me every time I looked at her. She had been riding double on the harness horse with me two years ago. Now she was a svelte young beauty, belle of the ball wherever she went. Young men admired her, courted her. The transition was too sudden for me. I surreptitiously watched her going out for a walk with her 'young man', fully expecting to see her any minute tuck her dress in her bloomers and hurdle over the post-and-rail fence; but no, she stood demurely to one side while the 'young man' let down the rail. It seemed to me that all the adventure that had been our life was ebbing swiftly away and that soon I too might be standing, hobbled by convention, waiting for a hand alien to our ways to let down the sliprail.

Mick hadn't chosen any of the acceptable young men who had jobs. She was going to marry Bob, the only one of her suitors who didn't have work – Bob, who could give her back just as much fight as she gave him. At first he had met with opposition from my family. He got around Mum with his good manners and respect for the elderly, two points by which Mum judged character. Dad was harder to get around; he had seen the effects of the Depression on men of good character.

'No man on the dole is immune to its rot,' he said. 'It destroys them all, the good and the bad.'

Mum once said, 'When it's all over and there are jobs for everyone then no one will be any the worse off for having been on the dole.'

'No man,' Dad said, 'who has ever been on the dole will ever again be the man he once was.'

'There's not enough work to keep a man alive,' Dad told Bob when he spoke for Mick. 'How do you expect to keep a wife as well?'

Bob quickly answered that on all jobs preference was given to married men.

'Have you got anything in kitty?'

'Nothing,' said Bob. 'But give me the green light and I'll change that.'

He had always got odd jobs because he was willing and strong. A day here, a day there, doing anything and everything, but the money he made would never add up to much. Shortly after this conversation with Dad, Bob had two days' work offered him on a saw bench in the railway yard near us cutting up condemned red-gum sleepers for firewood. From our end of the yard we could hear the big circular saw screaming all day. On the second day, just before knock-off time, the screaming stopped suddenly and in its place came a great booming like the tolling of a resonant bell. We ran outside and there was the sawmiller striking hell out of the big saw with an iron bolt to attract attention. Sitting in the sawdust at his feet was Bob, his hand held high in the air and blood streaming down his arm. His little finger was gone except for a few pieces of skin holding it to his hand, and they cut those off and drove him to Numurkah to the doctor.

'I don't know how it happened,' the sawmiller said. 'Never struck a man so good with the saw. Took to it like a duck to water. And he had to slip under it just before knock-off.'

'I suppose he earned his day's pay first?' Dad asked. When the owner nodded Dad said, 'Well, no one can say he isn't a trier.' He didn't oppose the marriage any longer.

Bob made only one slip that I know of about that accident. When the compensation money arrived he said, 'I thought it was £110 for the loss of a finger.'

'No,' Dad said dryly. 'You read the wrong section. Loss of the little finger only earns you £90.' It was enough for them to get married on and they stretched it out and it lasted them a long time.

When Mick turned nineteen Mum gave a party for her in the Waaia hall. No invitations were sent out, word was merely spread around that it was on. Eighty people turned up; some from outlying areas who couldn't get in sent gifts. There was a trestle table piled high with presents. Fettlers came and sleeper-cutters and wheat-buyers and farmers and retired people and the Aboriginal girl who worked at the hotel. Waaia had missed out on the division the Depression had brought to other places. There was no working class here, no gentry.

At the party Dad announced the engagement of Mick and Bob. Great shouts went up, cheers and good wishes.

'Gooda lucka,' called Chella Valenti, the wheat-lumper from southern Italy.

'We wish you both the best of luck,' said Mrs Tweddle, who would have been gentry anywhere else. Waaia was a wonderful place to live, all right.

Before the evening ended old Bill Leaf stopped the accordion-player to announce that there would be a kitchen tea in three weeks' time. 'Same place, same music.' And so it came to pass. They all rolled up again with gifts three weeks later and, as before, those who couldn't get in sent gifts – sets of saucepans, kitchen scales, cutlery, crockery, crystal, napery and cheques. They sang 'For they are jolly good fellows' to Bob and Mick and made speeches about both of them and about Mum and Dad. Speeches about Mick! The last speeches about her that I'd heard were to the effect that she'd come to a sticky end if she didn't give up riding crazy horses. Now it seemed she wasn't that same girl any more. She was a young lady and the men placed a chair for her when she wished to sit and held her coat for her. It was all very bewildering, and a little stab of self-pity came as I thought of myself as having been betrayed, deserted: Mick had gone over to the enemy, the adult world.

We went down to Gippsland for the wedding. On the way down Kevin was returned to his parents and I stayed with them for a time. Settling down in the Big Smoke, Melbourne, was an adventure of a different kind and Kevin and I went into it 'boots and all', as his grandfather said when we carted buckets of manure from a nearby dairy that used horses to pull their carts, and tipped it on the tiny pocket-handkerchief garden in front of the house. A policeman actually crossed the street one day to see what the smell was.

Kevin's father, whose neck had been broken when he arrived in the city, had been in plaster for half a year and only now was beginning to move around. Mrs Young had her dressmaking salon in the city. To teach us to find our way about Melbourne she suggested we should bring her lunch in each day using Kevin's bicycle for transport. We took it in turns 'dinking' one another and in a very short while knew all the short cuts, the back streets and the excitement of South Melbourne. But we were still bushwhackers to the backbone and after we'd been down in the city a full month, trying hard to lose our hayseeds, I said one night to Kevin when we were going to our bedrooms, 'Have you got the matches?' and he replied, 'I haven't even got the candle.' The electricity-conscious household loved telling this story.

Mick was married from Grandmother Adams's house with

me as bridesmaid and Mick's brother Jack as best man. The ceremony was simple, the wedding breakfast was simple, too, held in the big kitchen at Grandmother's house with the big Adams family gathered round. Grandmother bustled about, her plump little figure dainty and sweetly dressed, her white hair bunned on top, singing in her unaffected, pure voice, 'The Old Bullock Dray'. We all felt for a moment the nostalgia that had set her to singing that old bush song. She had been 'shown the bush' by her man all those long years ago when she'd accepted his invitation to 'step up and take possession of the old bullock dray.'

'Oh,' she said this day, 'young people have everything nowadays. When I was married you thought nothing of it if you had to sleep under the old bullock dray while you were waiting for your man to build your house.' Now she owned three cottages and land and was presiding over a table groaning with food, surrounded by her large family, most of whom had done well for themselves. I admired everything about this woman. She was the true pioneer, I knew. It was a pity that we were unable to communicate with one another. She never knew of my admiration; if she had any feeling for me beyond asperity I never knew it.

On our return from the church we changed our clothes. I had for my 'best' dress that white cotton I'd worn for the sports the year before when I'd won the egg and spoon race. To make it long enough for this year Mum had sewn a strip of material eight inches deep around the bottom. To relieve its starkness I tied a navy scarf with white spots around my neck. When she saw this, my grandmother spoke from her end of the table: 'That scarf makes you look very common, I must say.'

Tears blurred my sight, but I wouldn't let her humiliate me. I was too pig-headed for that.

'You're so anxious always to point out how common I am that I don't like to disappoint you,' I retorted. Inside I was sobbing. The wedding was all so lovely, the setting of the little cottage was perfect with its tecoma-covered walls; at the back, in an old shed almost hidden with flowers and creepers gone wild, the wedding gifts were displayed. I loved Mick. I thought I would never see a lovelier bride. Love, love, love. It was everywhere, but I knew one place where there was none for me. I tried not to let my unhappiness show by appearing nonchalant, uncaring, brazen. This led to reprimands from my aunts, all except aunt Anastasia Therese, that utterly fair person who never purposely hurt anyone. She called me Jeanne.

'Jeanne,' she told me, 'if you find you have inherited something no one in our family can understand, don't be afraid of it or try to suppress it. Don't worry about what people say. Be proud, never be afraid.' I couldn't understand her but I appreciated her kindness.

25

SCRIM WALLS

I t took a long time to get into bed at Grandmother Adams's. At home we dropped our clothes where we pulled them off and jumped in between the sheets that smelt of sunshine and ripening wheat crops, cuddled each other's backs to warm up and were asleep immediately. At Grandmother's it was different. Her bedroom was the most rarefied female room I've seen. I doubt that any man had set foot inside it. I was ten years old when Grandfather died and in all that time the two had occupied separate bedrooms. I once heard Grandmother reprimand my sister for flippantly showing her new husband some of her lingerie gifts.

'I've borne your grandfather ten children,' Grandmother said, 'and he's never so much as seen me in my petticoat.'

The very air in the room seemed to belie the presence of man on earth. I only once entered another room so rare, and that was at the convent; but here, in place of the simplicity of the convent room, was such a myriad of gew-gaws and lacy, frilly coverlets that there was virtually no part of the furniture, floor or walls on view. Starched white linen edged with lace covered everything even to the seat of the commode. Yet the room seemed, for all its accessories, strangely big and empty and cold after our warm, noisy, painted, cluttered-up room at home. Here we folded our clothes carefully and placed them in the sachets that had contained nightdresses by day and folded the many other gadget-holders and covers, and it all took time and during this time there invariably built up a sense of irrelation. It was like being an expatriate who has left behind him a warm, fruitful land and slowly finds that his new home is frigid, barren.

The only benefit of lying in this big, cold bed was that you could hear all the talk from the kitchen through the scrim walls, made of hessian covered with wallpaper. What I hadn't learned from the Marvels I picked up through those walls, because the grown-ups mostly talked of things that they could not mention when 'little pitchers have big ears' were around.

One night I heard Grandmother telling Mum about some neighbours. 'The daughter – well, she looked about fourteen and she had a miscarriage and the mother left home because of course as you might have guessed with a family where there'd been a divorce it was the father's, what more could you expect? And the father he fed the pigs . . .' I put my head under the blankets so as not to hear what was fed the pigs and then I lifted them so I could hear. Yes, the police had come and the people had moved.

These were the first people I had heard of who had been divorced, and the image the telling had impressed on my mind would have satisfied the most fanatical bigot. There was a lot to be learnt through those walls. I had heard enough through many nights of listening to know why Edna Ringer wore grey to her wedding.

'It was a nice little wedding,' Grandmother reported. 'She wore grey, of course.' Of course. Edna was a 'fallen woman'. She had had a child out of wedlock some years before when she was a young girl. The child was now in a foster home.

Dolly Sharp didn't wear grey. 'Rolled up to the church in a white dress as brazen as you like, veil and all. She must think we have short memories.' Some examples of this line of thought were so extreme that the sins of the mother could be visited on the daughter in the matter of a wedding dress.

'Margie wore an almost blue dress, not quite grey, quite a nice little outfit.' Her husband was disappointed that she had not worn white.

'They had to tell him and he took it like a man. "I'll marry her just the same," he said when they told him she was illegitimate.'

Another time they were talking about a young married woman who had had much difficulty at the time of the birth of her first child after marriage.

'Doctor found that she had stitches there. They'd been left in since the time she'd had a baby before marriage to teach her a lesson.' The aunt I didn't care for was talking.

'I think she got what she deserved.'

Because babies and allied subjects were taboo to most children in my circle until after marriage I didn't consider the morals involved in these sentiments, nor did I then recognise the fact that it is invariably the one with the most skeletons in the cupboard who shouts loudest about the mishaps of others and is the most unforgiving.

Most nights as the women talked there were sounds of cooking as a background, recipes being read aloud from Grandmother's hand-written recipe book, suggestions for improvements, the flip-flip of an egg whisk, the flop-flop of a hand beating sugar and shortening to cream in a big earthenware dish, the crunch of walnuts being shelled and the laughter as eyes ran with tears from the onions being peeled before they were pickled. Then the rattle of teacups.

A few nights after Mick's wedding they were making melon jam. I'd helped cut up the big, yellow, green-splotched melons before I went to bed. The big black seeds flew in all directions as we levered them out with the point of a knife. Such seeds are surprisingly slippery on a lino-covered floor, and when I was leaving the room to go to bed I slipped over on them. Grandmother laughed. I very stupidly took offence at being laughed at and stormed out without wishing anyone good night. I went to bed and lay there trying to think of a way I could go out and say good night without making it look like an apology for my behaviour.

They were talking about the melons, at least Mum was. She seemed to be talking feverishly, trying not to let Grandmother get a word in.

Eventually, 'Does she know?' Grandmother said, firmly. 'Have you told her?'

'No,' Mum replied.

'Well, you should tell her. She's getting far too big for her boots. She doesn't know her place.'

'Oh, I don't know . . .'

'I do. She'll turn out an upstart like her father if you don't watch out. You mark my words.'

'There'll be time enough later to tell her.'

'Tell her now.'

Mum said loudly, 'I won't. She's mine.'

'Don't be silly. She'll find out sooner or later that she's nothing to either of you.'

'She won't!' Mum was running outside and she shouted, 'She won't!'

My eyes were so wide open I couldn't focus properly on the shafts of moonlight coming in through the lace curtains. When Mum came to join me in the bed she put her arm around me. I pushed it off and moved away, lying stiff and motionless on the extreme edge of the bed, as far away from her as I could get.

In a while she whispered, 'Are you awake, Jeanie?'

There was no reply. Jeanie wasn't able to do as she wished any more. She had been swallowed up and was only a small part of the stranger who lay dry-eyed, numb, cold as stone in the bed.

Had anyone called out, 'Where's Jeanie?' I could have answered truthfully, 'She's not here.'

26

BLOOD
AND WATER

Not for a year did Mum speak to me of the things my grandmother had ordered her to speak of. Then she began diffidently, her words becoming muddled.

'I know,' I interrupted her, 'I know.' I walked out the kitchen door. She followed me.

'How do you know?'

'I've always known,' I lied.

She didn't speak of it again for a long time. Then, one day when I was cornered in the kitchen and couldn't get past her without actually pushing her away:

'Do you know who your parents are?'

'Of course.'

'You don't.'

I stared at her insolently, hoping to stop her. But she wouldn't stop.

'Don't you ever wonder?'

'No.' I had thought of it a little since that night, more in rage at their intrusion in my life and between Mum and Dad and me than from any desire to know them.

'You see your mother occasionally. She is one of my sisters.'

I wasn't interested. Mum thought this was a ruse, but it wasn't. I just didn't care.

'Blood is thicker than water,' Mum said. Fearfully she looked at me. 'Sometimes I've wondered if you haven't felt attracted to her rather than to me. It would be natural. Blood is thicker than water. Think of your aunts. Isn't there one you feel kin to?'

No, there wasn't. Suddenly: 'Not Auntie . . .?' I mentioned the one I was not particularly fond of.

'No.'

Thank goodness!

'She is one of my younger sisters.'

Good. It must be Aunt Sadie. I liked her tartness and incisive brain. She drove a semi-trailer in a trucking business with her husband.

So I tried to look casual. 'Is it Aunt Sadie?'

No, it wasn't. Mum was bewildered. 'I was sure you would know your own mother,' she said.

I longed to tell her not to be silly, that she was my mother. When she spoke the name of the woman who had borne me it moved me not at all.

'Oh, her,' I said.

'She and your real father,' Mum began, but I had heard enough and I pushed her aside and ran past her.

'If you want to get rid of me then I'm big enough to go,' I called back, cruelly, so she would realise she must say no more. She never mentioned it to me again. All I knew of my father were the barbed remarks I could remember from the past. I realised now that it was his decision not to spend the rest of his life with this family that made me, his child, the target for the barbs. I didn't care what he had done, whether it had been right or wrong; my only regret was that I had to know of it at all.

It was this knowledge and the constant whispering and the knowing looks whenever learning, art, music or books were mentioned that ended my childhood and made me uncertain for so long, made me look for love and affection when all the time I had it more than most will ever know. I remembered with hate the schoolteacher Louey Marsh hesitating over the name on my birth certificate: I had sensed something amiss that day; I was embarrassed when I thought of the kindness of that good man Kelly and his gang, at Nowingi, to the strange baby their mate had brought home; I thought of the many times I had been cruel and hurtful to Mum and Dad, taking for granted that I could hurt them because they were my parents; I thought of the times I'd complained to outsiders about Mum's restrictions, been disloyal to her.

As for religion, I no longer was fettered by it. I had striven to learn liturgical Latin in an endeavour to more fully participate in the service. But now I recalled a remark my crabbed aunt had passed, 'You and your fancy Latin. You're not even entitled to be a Catholic.' (*He* wasn't; whispers made it clear that he was a Freemason.) Now I thought of that remark as a passport to freedom. I was not bound to anything. I was free. I felt so free I longed for the chains of belonging to bind me tight again; but it was too late. I had fallen too hard.

'The bigger they are the harder they fall,' Dad used to shout above the noise of the Casey Jones on our Saturday morning trips. All the wheels of all the trains on all the journeys we had made never sounded so loud as the turmoil within my head.

27

THE CUP
OF KINDNESS

Dad began work again, but the heat of Waaia was too much for him and we must move to a cooler climate. This time we knew we were leaving Waaia forever. Mum went to her packing with a stolidity that was unusual in her.

'I think we'll have to get on with it, Birdie,' Dad had to gently remind her the day the trucks arrived at the siding to take on our goods. She wandered about, talking of the times we'd all sat up through the night with half our neighbours in the lounge listening to the Test match being played in England, amazed that we could hear such a thing from the other side of the world.

'Of course, it's all for the best,' she said brightly. We knew she didn't mean it any more than we did.

On my last day at school the fourteen children presented me

with a crystal powder bowl. I have never used it for fear that it might break.

'Goodbye, dreamer,' Mr Schmidt wrote on the card. 'Don't let them stop you from that. You're never beaten while you've a dream.' Ah yes, the dream, the beckoning finger. Gus Schmidt is dead now and my dream has vanished along with him.

The presentation to my parents in the Waaia hall was gay with music and dancing. Old Bill Leaf presented Dad and Mum with a most elegant canteen of cutlery and said that it was like seeing the horse-drawn wagons leave the roads to see the Smiths go from Waaia.

'You'll not be forgotten at Waaia,' he said. 'And we know you will not forget Waaia.'

They had us stand in the middle of the hall and they all stood about us in a circle and joined their hands.

'Oh no . . .' Mum said. They had already started to sing those words that must have wrenched more hearts than any others: 'Should auld acquaintance be forgot . . .' I didn't know till then why people weep when it is sung.

Next day the platform was crowded with people to watch the Smiths go. A royal send-off for a railway fettler and his family. We travelled in the guard's van; all our furniture was in the trucks ahead on the long goods train. At the last moment Mum remembered some instruction she had meant to leave for the new station-mistress who would come on the morrow; the fettlers came into the van for a last word with old Nip in his box with bars across the front.

The driver and guard didn't bustle us, but the time came when we must go. As the train began to roll, Bill Leaf on the platform called, 'Three cheers for Albert and family. Hip hip . . .' We waved from the windows in the van till they were out of sight. We had scarcely sat down when an explosion went off under the wheels, then another and another, bang bang bang as the wheels ran over the rails. It was detonators, used normally by the men to warn the guard of danger on the line. Now they put them along the track to farewell their mate on his way.

28

THE NEW LINE

Penshurst is in the Western District, a stony land twenty miles from Hamilton. This was the last part of our continent to settle down, and rocks from the time of upheaval haven't yet decayed. They lie around in such profusion that stone walls, houses, public buildings and miles of stone fences have been made with them. Penshurst itself grew up beside the crater of a dead volcano, Mount Rouse. It was quite a big town by the standards of anywhere else we had lived. There was a grocer, two butchers, a baker, a café, two hotels and two banks as well as – indication to us of its size – a railway station-master.

It was sheep country. The wealth of the district was in the score of sheep stations spread over the rocky volcanic country-side. There were no passenger trains through Penshurst, only steam-hauled goods trains. As at Monomeith the trucks on these trains were often the coaches of the job-hunters travelling down to the city or up the country looking for work. When the train with our furniture on board arrived I was watching Dad coming down the side of the track with his shovel on his shoulder, and as I watched his hand jerked imperceptibly upwards, the thumbs-up silent 'How are you, mate?' to a man peering from beneath the tarpaulin covering a truck.

We were a changed family now. Jack had gone to work in Gippsland and we were rarely to see him again in the future. Bob and Mick had come with us to Penshurst.

'There's sure to be plenty of work in such a big town,' Bob said in his optimistic way. Until he found this permanent job he and Mick were to live with us.

Bob was very good to me. He had had to leave high school when his people could no longer afford to keep him there. Now he encouraged me to go on with my plan for learning. We were further away from a high school here than we had been even at Waaia. Hamilton, twenty miles away, was the nearest and there was no transport even had we been able to afford it, which we couldn't.

I went along to the local State school. It was a big school, at least eighty children; a frightening rabble it seemed to me, used as I was to a maximum of twenty schoolmates. The headmaster could offer me no more than a desk if I wished to do correspondence lessons here.

I went home. 'I'd never learn quickly enough there,' I told Bob.

'What's the hurry?' he asked.

I had become a tense child in the past few months and had developed a tic in the lid of my right eye; it now began to twitch. I turned my back so that Bob would not see it, but he took me by the shoulders and turned me round.

'You're frightened,' he said.

'I'm never frightened,' I snapped.

'It's in your eyes. You've changed in the last few months.

You're lost.'

'I'm going to go away,' I told him. I hadn't known until then what it was I was going to do.

'What are you running away from?'

I didn't reply. My eye was shuttering up and down, I could feel the pull on my face muscles.

'Everybody loves you here.'

'Yes.' I knew that.

'Then why leave?'

I shook my head. I didn't know.

Money seemed scarcer than ever here, because of course there was more to spend it on. I went out to work. I was fourteen. At first I kept the books and did the accounts of a butcher, and in this way learnt the practical application of accounting; but such work could not fill my day now. As though smitten by some disease that gnawed the walls of the mind, exciting it to take in more and more, I applied myself to the limit. Calmly I set about studying whatever was available to me, without actually speaking of this to anyone, yet my urgency was such that it was conveyed to others. All sorts of people, unasked, offered to help me.

The town's policeman offered to teach me typing.

'I use two fingers,' he said, 'but I did learn to touch-type once and I'll teach you.'

Then I wanted to learn shorthand. 'I can't remember any of it, but I'll learn it again as I teach you,' he offered. Each day at 5 p.m. I'd tramp to the police station and apply myself to this dullest of all trades taught to women but, as I knew, one of the few occupations in business open to them.

The local priest offered to teach me Latin, surely the most beautiful of all languages. On Saturday mornings I'd cycle up to him for a two-hour lesson.

The correspondence lessons still came and these I did at night.

I had been learning music in a desultory manner for years from anyone who set up to be a teacher, but I had never had a good tutor. We had been at Penshurst for a few weeks only when

Mum came hurrying home from a Progress Association meeting.

'There's an excellent teacher comes here once a week,' she told me. 'I'll send you to her.'

Madame Sherman was not only talented, she was a fanatic. Music was her whole life.

'You'd better learn the violin too,' she told me. 'It will give you a wider appreciation of music.' She lent me a squeaky, cheap violin and each morning and evening as well as most of each weekend I practised these two instruments. (We had no near neighbours.) Under this musical martinet I sat the exams of the Music Examinations Board, the London College of Music, and the Trinity College of London, gaining diplomas from them all for the piano and advanced passes for the violin and theory. In one month, May 1939, I sat for and passed five examinations. I was as indefatigable as Madame. We punished one another with our perseverance and labour.

Because the work I had begun was tedious and because I wanted to earn more money than the fifteen shillings a week offered for book-keepers, as well as wanting to have more time to study, I set up in business on my own, a freelance you might say. Mum advanced me the money for a secondhand typewriter and with this I tendered to do the monthly accounts of three shops – two butchers and a baker. I arranged that I was to work when and for as long as I pleased so long as I had the accounts out by the first of each month. At 'peak' periods such as Friday nights and Christmas week I worked for a newsagent, a fine chinaware shop, and served at the bakery.

But the best means of earning money was playing in the dance band. The New Mayfair Dance Band was, when I was invited to join, composed of four cool sophisticated male musicians. I still wore my school clothes, my hair was dressed in shoulder-length curls, I wore cotton stockings and lace-up shoes. Our engagements were usually only on Saturday nights at the local hall, but during the shearing season we'd get several bookings from the shearing sheds for 'cut out' dances, the social event of the sheep country year, held in the cleaned-up shed to celebrate

172

the end of the shearing on each station. Dressing was formal, the women in floor-length gowns, and a certain distinction was lent by the presence of an 'official party' consisting of the matron of the local hospital (to which proceeds from the dance were donated), the doctor, squatters and their wives, a bank manager or two, and the local councillors. But all this respectability could not dampen a shearers' hop and it was the bales of wool set around the walls for seats that set the atmosphere for the evening. Sometimes they danced until dawn. We were paid to play until 2 a.m.

The first 'cut out' ball I played at was in a shearing shed near Coleraine. At 2 a.m. the shearers decided the evening had only then begun so they started to take the hat around.

'We must keep the orchestra,' they said.

When the hat came to him, a smart 'gun' said, 'Aw, b— that!' and slapped a ten shilling note on top of the old piano. Half a dozen followed suit. The little pile of money shook and trembled there near me all the while I played. At the end of the long night we musicians would share it. I knew I would have at least £2 to take home to Mum.

These young musicians were kind to me. Although my mother insisted on my appearing dressed as a child (as indeed I was), these boys knew I was dance-mad and when they'd see a young shearer look at me they'd call to him, 'Why don't you ask her for a dance?' and they'd play while I danced. But the moment the dance ended they shepherded me back into their midst like clucky hens.

The best shearers were often the best dancers and almost always the best dressed, but they were also likely to be the wildest. Sometimes, dancing by the big, open doors at the end of the shed, you could see white shirt-tails flapping as men fought in the light of the big fire built of tree trunks. One night my partner told me that there were three fights going at the same time and that four of the fighters were 'gun' shearers.

I was book-keeping, studying piano and violin, learning Latin, taking six school subjects, playing in the dance band, and now

I took music pupils. I was a good piano tutor, but I was not a meticulous book-keeper and I was constantly employed thinking up quick answers to irate customers. But it was all worth it. One week during which I played with the dance band for two engagements I brought home £6 from my various projects. Mum bought herself a new pair of lace-up corsets and the sight of those formidable stays filled me with pride.

At this time we lost a dear friend. Old Nip, the dog, who for so long had been one of the family, died at last. He was as old as I was, which was old for a dog, but still he went to work on the Casey and trotted slowly down the track after Dad.

This morning when Dad called him as he went out the gate on his way to work the old dog didn't respond. Dad went round to his kennel. The dog's head barely lifted at his approach.

'Hey, you old scoundrel. Have you gone on strike?' Dad said. There was fear in his voice as he put out his hand to pat the old head. 'Come on, boy!' he said, and whistled. But the dog couldn't rise. His beautiful brown eyes were opaque with pain.

'Poor old feller,' Dad said. 'My poor old mate.'

He tried to help him, but the dog was beyond help. He went then and got a gun from Joe Page, a fettler.

Mum put her arms round me and we went inside. Dad picked the grizzled old dog up in his arms and carried him down the line away from the town.

BOB'S MATE

Historians say that the Depression ended before the war broke out, but for the men who needed work the Depression was still on, even if it had ended for the financiers. Dad was a ganger now and we knew how badly men wanted jobs.

One night of that year, 1939, Gus Schramm knocked on our door. It was late, but I was up studying so I answered the knock. Gus saw me come out in the lamplight and jumped back into the shadows near the garden gate; he had not expected anyone other than Dad to be up. I was scared and backed into the passage-way.

His voice spoke from the darkness, 'Get your Dad, Smithy.'

'Dad,' I bawled. 'Dad! There's a man in the garden.'

Dad came out and put his arm around my shoulders. He was not a big man and since the accident was thin like a shoe-lace, but he was as strong as ever and radiated security. He went to the door casually, leading me beside him, calming my panic with ease.

'How are you, mate?' he said out into the silent dark. The way my father spoke was an assurance of goodwill.

Gus responded and stepped closer, but he kept to the shadows like a guilty man; and Gus was guilty. He had come to do his best friend, my brother-in-law Bob, out of his job.

He blurted out his shame to my father. 'It's two years since I've had work. There's the kids . . .' he said. He had three. 'There's another on the way. I want Bob's job.'

Dad knew what Gus's next remark would be. He had waited to hear it from someone ever since he had given the job to Bob two weeks before. Now it was Gus who said it.

'Bob's got a finger missing. Government regulations for his job say you can't employ a man with his finger missing.'

Men working on the job for a long time might know this, but Gus was young and had never worked for a Government concern – how would he know?

'Who told you?' Dad asked.

Gus hesitated, then said abruptly, as though shame had sped with his pride, 'Bob told me.'

'When?'

'Tonight, on his way home from work. We had a yarn. He was afraid someone would find out about it.'

Dad said, 'So he told you, his mate.' Gus didn't answer that. After a while he said, 'Will I start in the morning?'

Dad was holding me very tightly around the shoulders. I thought he was angry but he only sounded very tired when he spoke. 'Why are you so sure you'll get the job?'

Gus's answer was logical, final. He even stepped from the shadows into the lamplight as he replied.

'Because I was the first to apply for it after Bob was put off.'

Probably it was only a second, but it seemed like a very long

176

time they stood there looking at one another. They didn't speak, but after a while Gus turned and stumbled towards the gate. Dad, with his arm still about my shoulder, turned and went into the house.

Bob was twenty-two, my sister nineteen, and their first baby was only three months away. This, Bob had thought, was the permanent job he was always speaking of getting.

Dad went into their room and wakened Bob.

'I've got bad news,' he said. Bob held up his hand, the one with only four fingers, and Dad nodded. Bob asked who had come with the accusation.

'Never seen him before,' Dad said. Bob asked if Dad had given the informer the job. Dad shook his head.

Quickly Bob said, 'Then lend me your bike. I'll nick round and give Gus the tip before word gets round. He needs work bad and he'd have done the same for me if things had been different.'

'Yes,' said Dad. 'He would have if things had been different.'

And the money from that little finger was all gone now.

The Western District was hard hit at this time. There were no factories here, no mills, few farms. The large sheep stations in the district had permanent staff. Even their rabbit-trappers were permanent. There was nothing here for men looking for work but the dole. It was this that had driven Gus to take Bob's job.

Now that he was out of work again Bob was free to wander the streets, hold up the verandah post of the pub, or wander idly to the billiard room, but he never became apathetic about being unemployed. He was always optimistic: something would turn up. He had a go at anything. He even learnt to knit, and to pay for his keep at home he made clothes for dozens of dolls Mum was dressing for distribution to needy children that Christmas. They were fiddling little dresses, and minute booties and bonnets that tied under the dolls' chins with narrow ribbon. Bob's big, calloused hands were clumsy at first, but by the time he was finished every doll was perfect because he unravelled all his work until it was just right and, as he said, the calluses soon disappeared when a man was out of work. He prowled the town every day keeping his eyes and ears open and picked up lots of odd jobs. He was one of the first to hear that a contractor was coming to open up the old quarries to get metal out for a road job. This meant that he was in the first gang to start work there.

So many men applied that the contractor offered two days a week to each man to split it up fairly. But that only lasted two weeks. On the first day of Bob's second ration of work Bluey Turner was killed. We knew about it in the town because someone rang the Catholic church bell. We all ran up to see what the trouble was.

The priest said, 'The overhang at the quarry has fallen in and buried poor Bluey Turner alive. They want him dug out, quick.'

All the men and boys raced off on bikes and trucks and the shops and the hotel shut because all the men had gone. There had been little equipment at the quarry to move rock and earth; little was needed when there were so many hands anxious for work. They tried to save Bluey with their bare hands, scrabbling into the sharp stones and heaving boulders aside.

During the afternoon another cave-in immediately above them nearly trapped the men who were digging, and the police ordered them away until the overhang could be shored up. By now it was too late. The second fall had brought down piles of rubble on top of the great pile on the body of Bluey, who they now knew must be dead. Still they worked on through the night. Lanterns swung from forked sticks stuck in the rubble and car headlights blazed on them. When daylight came they began to work in relays.

It was 10 a.m. when the flat-topped truck came rumbling down the main street with the last shift on board. Sitting round the outside edge of the tray, with their legs in heavy boots dangling over the side, cigarettes hanging off their lips, the men formed a barricade hiding the tarpaulin-covered mound in the centre of the tray.

They placed Bluey in a clean stable at the hotel until the

inquest and then they buried him, and all the boys of the town turned up to walk behind the old hearse because they had nothing else to do. They were out of work again now the quarry had closed.

Bob had made furniture for the expected baby, a cot and a tiny table and chair all fashioned from packing cases with the rough wood sandpapered so smooth you could rub your hand over it and it felt like silk. But my sister wanted a pram.

'And,' she warned, 'I don't expect to push a packing case on wheels up the street either! I want a proper pram, a bought pram.'

So Bob left home and said he wasn't coming back until he had enough money for a bought pram.

'I'm going rabbiting,' he announced. He took Whacko the dog, Dad's bike and some borrowed traps and disappeared for three weeks. All that was visible when he returned was his face grinning in triumph; the rest of him was rabbit skins, bike and all, skins strung inside out on wire frames.

They went up to town the next day, Bob with his skins bound tightly in a bundle, Mick to wait at the post office until he returned with the money. Then they would buy the pram. We watched them go, laughing like the kids they were, Bob teasing Mickie that he could not walk with his arm around her waist any more because she no longer had a waist, and she laughingly threatening to box his ears. After they had gone a little way they held hands. They looked good. Their happiness in one another and the whole world around them that day came back to us watching them go up the road to buy the pram.

I had not truly seen the face of the Depression until I saw those two coming home that day. The Depression was something that had happened to other people, not us, I thought. But its ugly face came down that road with those two who didn't look like kids any more. Bob didn't hold Mickie's hand, they didn't even walk side by side. Instead, Bob strode out, hands in pockets, intent it seemed on the straggly gums at the roadside. Mickie was walking a few paces ahead of him, striding out a little faster than him, even though she was pregnant, and she was whistling. She looked 'brassy', as we used to call cheap girls then. Mum and Dad and I stood at the kitchen window watching them come.

'What does that girl think she's up to?' Mum said disapprovingly, and she pushed up the window to tell my sister to behave herself. Dad stopped her.

'Leave them alone,' he said. 'Come away from the window. Don't let them know we've been watching for them.' Dad knew what had happened.

'I reckon the dealers wouldn't buy Bob's skins. I thought they mightn't. He had them pegged out wrongly.'

Buyers could pick and choose in a period when it seemed that every second man in creation was out rabbiting.

I don't think Bob ever mentioned those skins to anyone. Mick didn't either. He went to the council chambers the next day and signed the form to go on the dole. He had never done that before. It was as though he had come to the end of a long passage-way of hope and found there was nothing there after all his striving.

They moved from our house and took a tiny cottage out of town. Mum begged them to stay, at least until the baby was born, but Bob said, 'We've got to face it, Mum. We've got to make it or break it alone.'

He was resigned, but resignation and unbounded optimism can go hand in hand when you're young – along with high spirits. The high spirits of him and a score of other young dole boys in the town bubbled up in April of that year, 1939, when they crept out at midnight and decorated the war memorial on Anzac eve with cabbages they stole from the priest's garden.

'I don't see what the caterwaulin's all about,' the old Irishman said the next day when the 'desecration' was being decried all over town.

'After all, they were my cabbages, and I'm not complaining. If it gave the boys a bit of fun, surely they get little enough of it.'

I wonder if any of the citizens of that little town ever look at the new names on the ugly little stone memorial and remember the boys who prematurely decorated their own tombstone that year with cabbages. Bob's name is there now and Gus Schramm's too, and numbered among the other names are most of the lads who drew the dole with Bob in those other hungry years.

THE
LAST DANCE

I n June 1939 there was to be a debutante ball. Mum was
working for its success. There was to be a sit-down turkey
and ham supper, a Melbourne dance band, a bishop for the
debs to be presented to, and a real 'Lady' to do the presenting.

I had never seen a presentation of debutantes. I hoped I could
go, short dress and all. I decided to work on Dad.

'It would be the first time I've ever been to such a dance,'
I said.

'It might be the last,' Dad said. He was preoccupied with
world news.

Mum looked at me reflectively. 'It would be a pity if you
never had a chance to wear a long dress,' she said.

And so while I was still a child I was presented to the Bishop of Ballarat. Next in age to me was a girl of eighteen. Most of the others were in their twenties. And, as Dad had predicted, it was to be my last chance to take part in this insane but delightful ceremony.

The other debs couldn't dance well. Some of them had had lessons for a few weeks before the ball. None of them knew that I had been taught by the best dancers the bush had bred, and I'm sure they all hated me very much as the evening wore on and the best dancers in the hall swooped down on me. The boys from the New Mayfair Dance Band would of course recognise my partners – all the gun shearers were in town for the big ball.

Never did I know such a night: the music, the dancing, my first long dress, the flowers, the attention. All too soon the band played 'Goodnight, sweetheart', the last quickstep; it was always, 'Goodnight, sweetheart, goodnight'.

It was the evening of Sunday, 3 September. We sat in front of the fire listening to the radio. The old wireless with the big flower-like trumpet had gone; this was the latest model. But we had never listened so intently, not even when we listened to our first broadcast back in the old days.

All afternoon Dad had sat in the house waiting for this. He said abruptly when we began to fool, 'Keep quiet!' Mick and Bob were visiting and we sobered, hearing Dad severe one of the few times in our lives. Then the message came through. The static crackled but the words were clear. We were at war.

Not one of us spoke until after the playing of 'God Save the King' had ended. They had never done that before. In a play or speech, whenever he heard the call 'Three cheers for the King!' Dad would grin and we knew he was thinking of his navy days when the traditional lower-deck reply was 'Bugger the King!' Now he stood for the playing of the anthem, leaning on the mantelpiece, looking into the fire so that it would not seem affected.

I was growing up and life was now, not later, and right now

there was to be a Sunday dance in the church hall and Dad had promised to take me for a short while. Now there was no doubting by the way he stood that we were not going.

Mickie broke the silence: 'They'd never take married men.'

Bob sat on the arm of her chair. 'It's a job,' he said, his voice serious, but his eyes betraying him. All the boredom, the lethargy and despondency had gone. They scintillated with excitement.

Bob and his mates were standing at the street corner the following day when the newspaper truck came in. They had heard the announcement on the radio, but this was different. The written word was the seal to the statement and there it was, on the poster on the side of the truck. One word. War.

Within a month there was hardly a young man left in the town. The boys were all 'jumping the rattler' in one direction now: Bob and his mates were on their way to the city to enlist.

Many of Australia's Sixth Division men had been on the dole. That's the way Bob and the boys like him got their first really permanent job.

In my own private world that I had thought was all the world I had been muddling on. Now there was no need for decisions. I was sheathed with patriotism. I had heard the band play and like the soldier who had spoken at that Anzac Day commemoration which I had been thrashed for attending, I had fallen in behind the music. I would go to this war. Even to bob and float in the little whorls and eddies on the perimeter of this holocaust would be adventure enough to make my nameless, faceless fears insignificant.

To my already numerous occupations were added first-aid and home-nursing lectures and four hours a week working as nurses' aide in the local hospital. I had joined the VADs and must have a first-aid and a home-nursing certificate as well as one hundred hours' nursing experience before I could enlist. I liked the hospital training although it consisted mainly of 'Shut your eyes and tip', advice from the training sister on the task which was for the next three years to be almost my entire contribution to the war effort – emptying pans and bottles.

Before I left for my first posting my two grandmothers had died. Granny Smith, to quote her son, the prodigal Ted, 'died of cantankerousness'.

It was a cold, frosty winter and one morning she insisted on going down the outside stairs, 'for a breath of fresh air', as she said. She was warned that the steps were iced over, but as soon as she found herself alone took her stick and went out. She was lying on the ground when they came in answer to her cry, her hip fractured. The ninety-six-year-old bone wouldn't mend. She lingered a little time in hospital.

'She won't let us take her corsets off,' matron told Mum when she arrived. She was old and crippled, but all the strong young nurses couldn't wrest the old lace-ups from her.

'Why won't you let the nurses take your corsets, Gran?' Mum asked.

The old lady beckoned her close to her lips and whispered, 'I've got my money sewn up in them.'

'You're just a mean old Scotswoman,' Mum teased her.

'I'm not mean, Birdie,' Gran said. 'I'm canny.'

She allowed Mum to take off her corsets on condition she placed them under her pillow.

When she was going Mum asked, 'Can I leave you some silver to buy some fruit, Gran?'

'I don't want any fruit,' she said. 'But you can leave the silver if you like.' She laughed a lot over that. 'Remember what I used to tell Jeanie. Take what you're offered and look around for more.' And she chuckled again. The following day she died.

Grandmother Adams took a stroke and lay for a weary time dying in her trim white bed. I spent some time in the house when she was dying. As she fought for life I began to see the battle she had fought all her life, the battle for what she thought was right and moral. In her way she had tried to avenge what she considered were wrongs.

Perhaps we all do a bit of that, unaware that the battleground of life is not laid out with the opponents facing one another. It is more a vague, ephemeral, unfenced arena that has no boundaries; we can't recognise the enemy and great clouds roll over, preventing us from seeing clearly; a field in which the most we can hope to do is parry the thrusts as they come at us through the swirling mists that, often as not, hide the hand that holds the weapon.

As I watched Grandmother Adams silently battling there on the narrow white bed I lost my fear of her, and an understanding akin to love came in its place. She neither spoke nor opened her eyes. There was no way of telling if she were conscious. She could neither eat nor drink. One day the doctor came to examine her and he drew the bedclothes down and raised her nightdress to use the stethoscope on her heart. With the faintest of movements her tiny hands pushed the gown down, modestly covering her body. Then she folded her hands again with the rosary beads clasped in her fingers. Sometimes we found the beads had been moved along as though she followed the prayers constantly being chanted in her room.

Her sister-in-law, my great-aunt Anastasia Byrnes, herself quite an old lady, had been with her all the time of her dying. When the time came that it must end she placed Grandmother's left hand in the brown shroud she had had ready in the dresser in her bedroom for many years. In the other hand she placed a lighted candle. It was an hour of sombre dignity. My great-aunt Anastasia sat there until the end, bridging the gulf between life and death. When Grandmother breathed no more the candle was extinguished.

Within a short time of one another, these, my two grand-mothers, were lowered into the soil where grew neither the thistle nor the shamrock, yet soil that was richer for their having laboured over it.

One obvious snag to my enlisting was my age or, to be more precise, my lack of age. This was overcome quite simply by coaxing Mum to sign the permission for me to join up and filling in the details later, in private.

'But will they take girls so young?' my mother asked. I was nearly seventeen.

'Oh yes,' I assured her. 'Look at the civilian hospitals. They had me training there.'

And then I was off, heading for Spencer Street, weighted down with the accoutrements of that war I'd not given a moment's thought to except as its being a vehicle by which I might escape from the turmoil in my mind. My peace did not come in a flash, a moment of light like the opening of a third eye. Rather, confidence stole back into me in its own sweet, meandering time. But this day saw the beginning of it as we jostled on that crowded platform.

We were not a homogeneous group yet; we hadn't rid ourselves of the secret life each of us had left behind, but we had one binding thing in common: we belonged to Australia, to the very soil of Australia. Half the population still lived in rural areas, the bush; the other half, though urban, was rural-minded, knew that the country still rode on the sheep's back, that our wealth came from what our land and our men made together. Whatever we were, the soil had made us. In the first world war and now this one, Australia had sent away armies notorious for their lack of discipline but famous for the bush-bred initiative that makes formal discipline unnecessary.

We were all here on this train, every one of us, but the drift to the cities had already begun and Australia would never see the likes of us again. If patriotism was only sheathed on me until that day it commenced now to grip my marrow.

'Do you know Spencer Street railway station?' the kindly matron had asked. Surely. It was my stamping ground, the city arena where we'd swaggered in pride in being bush-bred. Mothers soothe a fretful child with play-talk: 'Hear the train blow, love?' imitating the whistle of a steam engine. But me, I'd heard the real train blow, and spent a childhood steeped in the essence of all those things that condense and issue forth from the banshee-like wail of roaring, rushing engines. I'd slept twelve feet from the rails, heard the wheels crunch by like nailed boots crossing my bedroom floor, listened to the whistle shrieking and fading past our many outback homes, houses made into homes because wherever Mum and Dad got off the wallaby was home to us.

I'd shared in the camaraderie of people working hard and playing with gusto. Others may speak of the 'working class'. We were aristocrats. We had a whole town turn out to bid us farewell.

'Three cheers for Albert and family,' they'd called. I'd seen the passing parade crystal clear, because that's the way my parents had seen it – yes, my parents, for if the love and the lack of humbug in my life had taught me one thing it was to recognise the value of people, places and things. Now I began to see that there was no dilemma. If others wanted to weigh themselves down with whispers and aged feuds, that was their burden, not mine. I'd had everything. None could have had better.

EPILOGUE

D ad lived until February 1980, loving, lively, witty, gentle, dignified, tough of body – working with his pick and shovel on the roads of Buln Buln Shire until he was seventy-five years of age. Mum lived until her ninety-third year and we buried the dear lady near her birthplace in Buln Buln. Miss Mickie is still very funny and still doesn't give a damn for anybody.

Mr Schmidt, my old teacher from Waaia, wrote to me before he died. 'I heard there was a book,' he said. 'I left the school and began to run and in the newspaper shop in the little town I was in I said, "I want the book" and they knew what it was, because they had read it. And I told them I knew you'd do it. I've got my notes of those days to prove I always knew it.'

Nuns, now elderly, who encouraged me in such abandoned liberties when I was foisted on them, have written. 'I laughed and laughed,' wrote one nun, 'at your thinking we were all bald!' Another said, 'We pray for you here in our little chapel at Numurkah.' (I wasn't too sure about that, but Mum said that though you may not see any good it does, you just think of the harm it might have saved you from.)

Joe Page, the Penshurst fettler, telephoned when Dad died. 'What can I do to help? I owe a lot to your father. He gave me a job in the Depression, took me into his gang. Rescued me and mine. What can I do?' Old Constable Golding when he came to my parents' Diamond Wedding in 1979 asked 'And have your outlines improved?' of the shorthand he'd taught me forty years before. And listening to Mum and the old man talking I learnt that it was he who bought my first typewriter that set me up as a small-town tycoon.

Sir Ronald East remembered our paths crossing in the other days. He built the iron-clad water catchment at Nowingi near our home, an innovative attempt to try to trap water from the arid lands; he flew over our home and waved to the two little girls on the platform at Monomeith when we were marooned by the flood-waters and we waved back to him. If only we had known we were waving to a pilot who'd been with the Australian Flying Corps in World War I! To the man who was to become Chairman of the State Rivers and Water Supply Commission! Oh, 'a real big-wig'! Wouldn't we have been impressed! Actually, no. All we wanted was for the pilot to believe that we were poor little waifs abandoned in the midst of the swirling yellow flood-waters. We were most terribly dramatic.

Readers write to say they have visited Waaia after reading the book and many send me photographs they have taken of the still-small settlement. Waaia boys who had it rough in those hard days are now sporting wide-brimmed hats in keeping with their wide acres, because irrigation has come to their stunted holdings; they look me up when they come down to the city for the Show and it's grand to see them getting some good years under their belts.

The Mallee is quite unlike we knew it. It is now the olive-green it was before the big rollers cleared it. No farming is permitted on the marginal lands where the soldier settlers broke their hearts, and the scrub has grown again. There are no dust storms – and Melbourne housewives no longer rush to bring the washing in off the line as they had to do when they saw the red clouds of dust drop from the sky in the 1920s and 1930s. The Sunset Country is still a blank space on the map, with Government Bore or Pink Lakes (Salt) marked where there are no roads.

No place we lived in is as we knew it. There is not one station left standing where Mum was station-mistress and Dad folded the big tarpaulins off the trucks for her at night; our homes have gone, every one, with the tank-stands made of sleepers where the tin dish stood for our daily wash, and gone too are the wash-houses where we boiled the copper; there are no trucks in the sidings where we played in the golden days and fettlers travel to work by car and drive labour-saving machines where Dad and his mates toiled with their 28-pound hammers to straighten the rails. 'For all the good old fettlers are buried out on the hillside,' as an old railway song goes.

In some ways it is as though we never lived. There is no monument to the toilers of a land and they wouldn't expect it. But a nation will be poorer if it forgets them.

Patsy Adam-Smith is one of Australia's best-known and best-loved authors. Awarded the OBE in 1980 and the AO in 1994, she has had thirty-one books published, all of which have either topped or been featured on the best-seller lists of their time. *The Anzacs* was joint winner of the Age Book of the Year award in 1978, and *Prisoners of War* received the Order of Australia Association Book Prize in 1993.

OTHER WORKS BY PATSY ADAM-SMITH

Rediscovering Tasmania: the North-West Coast (1955), with Piet Maree
Moonbird People (1965)
There Was a Ship (1967)
Tiger Country (1968)
Hobart (1968), with Max Angus
The Rails Go Westward (1969)
Folklore of the Australian Railwaymen (1969)
Across Australia by Indian–Pacific (1971)
No Tribesman (1971)
Port Arthur (1971), with Max Angus
Tasmania (1971), with Max Angus
Footloose in Australia (1973)
Romance of Australian Railways (1973)
The Barcoo Salute (1973)
Launceston (1973), with Max Angus
The Desert Railway (1974)
Trader to the Islands (1977)
The Anzacs (1978)
Islands of Bass Strait (1978)
Victorian and Edwardian Melbourne from Old Photographs (1979)
Romance of Victorian Railways (1980)
Outback Heroes (1981)
The Shearers (1982)
When We Rode the Rails (1983)
Australian Women at War (1984)
Heart of Exile (1986)
Australia, Beyond the Dreamtime (1987), with Thomas Keneally and Robyn Davidson
Prisoners of War: From Gallipoli To Korea (1992)
Trains of Australia (1993)
Goodbye Girlie (1994)